The World's Greatest
HOTELS

2014 EDITION

TRAVEL+
LEISURE
BOOKS

AMERICAN EXPRESS PUBLISHING,
A DIVISION OF TIME INC. AFFLUENT MEDIA GROUP.
NEW YORK

A lounge at Aman Canal Grande, in Venice.

The World's Greatest
HOTELS

2014 EDITION

Introduction by Nancy Novogrod

**TRAVEL+
LEISURE
BOOKS**

AMERICAN EXPRESS PUBLISHING CORPORATION,
A DIVISION OF TIME INC. AFFLUENT MEDIA GROUP.
NEW YORK

Travel+Leisure
The World's Greatest Hotels
Ninth Edition

Editor Clara O. Sedlak
Consulting Editor Laura Begley Bloom
Art Director Phoebe Flynn Rich
Photo Editor Zoey E. Klein
Production Associate Andre Bassuet
Assistant Editors Nate Storey, Aarti Virani
Contributing Editor Jaime Gillin
Copy Editors David Gunderson, Mimi Hannon,
Mike Iveson, Edward Karam, Pablo Morales,
Libby Sentz, Suzan Sherman
Researchers Kyle Avallone, Stephanie Sonsino

TRAVEL+LEISURE
Editor-in-Chief Nancy Novogrod
Design Director Sandra Garcia
Executive Editor/Content Strategist Jennifer Barr
Managing Editor Laura Teusink
Associate Managing Editor Patrick Sheehan
Arts/Research Editor Mario R. Mercado
Copy Chief Kathy Roberson
Photo Director Scott Hall
Production Manager Ayad Sinawi
Associate Research Editor Tomás Martín

**AMERICAN EXPRESS PUBLISHING, A DIVISION
OF TIME INC. AFFLUENT MEDIA GROUP**
President and Chief Executive Officer Ed Kelly
**Chief Marketing Officer and President,
Digital Media** Mark V. Stanich
CFO, SVP, Corporate Development and Operations
Paul B. Francis
VP, General Managers Frank Bland, Keith Strohmeier
VP, Books and Products Marshall Corey
Director, Books Programs Bruce Spanier
Senior Marketing Manager, Branded Books
Eric Lucie
Director of Fulfillment and Premium Value
Philip Black
**Manager of Customer Experience and Product
Development** Betsy Wilson
Director of Finance Thomas Noonan
Associate Business Manager Uma Mahabir
VP, Operations Tracy Kelliher
Operations Director Anthony White

Cover: Lounging on a deck at El Nido Resorts in Palawan, Philippines. Photographed by Francisco Guerrero.

Back cover, from top: The lobby at the Langham, Chicago; a villa at Awasi Patagonia, in Chile; a guest room at Alma Hotel & Lounge, in Tel Aviv. Photographed by Kevin J. Miyazaki (top); courtesy of Awasi Patagonia (middle); Sivan Askayo (bottom).

ISBN 978-1-932624-65-6

Published by American Express Publishing, a division of Time Inc. Affluent Media Group
1120 Avenue of the Americas
New York, New York 10036

AMERICAN EXPRESS PUBLISHING is a trademark of American Express Marketing & Development Corp. and is used under limited license. Time Inc. Affluent Media Group is not affiliated with American Express Company or its subsidiaries. TRAVEL + LEISURE is a trademark and registered trademark of Time Inc. Affluent Media Group.

Distributed by Charlesbridge Publishing
85 Main Street, Watertown, Massachusetts 02472

Printed in the U. S. A.

A guest tent at Erg Chigaga Luxury Desert Camp, in Morocco.

A poolside stroll at Lake Austin Spa Resort, in Texas.

Contents

contents

KEY $ *Less than $200* $$ *$200 to $350* $$$ *$350 to $500* $$$$ *$500 to $1,000* $$$$$ *More than $1,000*

Arts and Crafts–
style gardens off
Barnsley House,
in England.

KEY   **$** *Less than $200*   **$$** *$200 to $350*   **$$$** *$350 to $500*   **$$$$** *$500 to $1,000*   **$$$$$** *More than $1,000*

contents

9

The pool
at Casa Chic,
in Uruguay.

contents

A guest room at
Alma Hotel &
Lounge, in Tel Aviv.

Introduction

Even in New York City, where I live, hotels are a happily unavoidable part of my life. Mornings often start out at the Lambs Club, Geoffrey Zakarian's restaurant in the Chatwal Hotel, which along with Sirio's at the Pierre is one of my frequent haunts for breakfast meetings. My haircuts take place at the Carlyle, where I visit Yves Durif's salon each month; and on weekdays you would have found me in the Loews Regency gym by 7 a.m., until it closed for renovations in December of 2012 (it reopened to much fanfare this January). The gym, alas, is now for guests only, but the restaurant and take-out coffee shop have eased their way onto my itinerary.

In a single year, T+L profiles thousands of hotels and resorts, and our editors and reporters vet at least twice as many more. The ninth annual edition of *The World's Greatest Hotels* showcases a richly varied lot, from a mountain hideaway in Bhutan's Paro Valley to a majestically restored Russian palace in St. Petersburg and an haute-luxury reinvention of a classic Puerto Rican beach resort.

That all of these properties offer up authentic experiences of their locations—whether platters of bivalves plucked from the waters near the Oyster Inn on Waiheke Island, in New Zealand; a private blending session with a renowned winemaker at Casa de Uco, in the Andean foothills; or rooms lined in volcanic rock at the Monaci delle Terre Nerre, in Sicily, a tribute to nearby Mount Etna—is a reflection of their distinctly modern flavor. In today's world, travel dreams are so often about encounters with the local and real.

What separates a pleasant stay from a memorable one so often resides in less tangible, human elements—the attention to detail and expert service provided by the staff: the personal travel attaché at the Quin, in New York City, who can arrange for an after-hours tour of the Guggenheim Museum; or housekeeping at the Banyan Tree Shanghai on the Bund, which discreetly picks up laundry for same-day service from a valet box by your door; or butlers who hand-deliver chocolate truffles at the Oberoi Dubai. It's these gracious touches that can imprint a hotel stay on your memory.

Carefully curated by *Travel + Leisure*'s editors, who spend months selecting properties to be included, this volume highlights the judgments of the magazine's well-traveled readers as well, who speak out through the results of our annual World's Best Awards survey and T+L 500, both of which are featured in the final section. These lists spotlight what our readers love now, including far-flung safari camps, high-design urban escapes, and classic resorts. Beyond that, there's an index that will allow you to search for properties by location and category, from family-friendly to eco-chic.

My own next stops: India and Sri Lanka. As always, I'll be on the lookout for hotels that deliver comfort, the opportunity for discovery, and a distinctive—and enchanting— sense of place.

Nancy Novogrod EDITOR-IN-CHIEF

The living room at the Lake Austin Spa Resort, in Austin, Texas.

United States
+ Canada

A lighthouse on the Atlantic shore near North Haven, Maine.

Dinner at Nebo Lodge. Above: A house-made-pickle plate.

NORTH HAVEN, MAINE

Nebo Lodge

Sometimes a single hotel can put a relatively unknown destination on the map—and so it was with Nebo Lodge and the three-mile-wide Penobscot Bay island of North Haven, an hour's ferry ride from Rockland. The nine-room property has all the trappings you'd expect from a classic New England island escape—gray wainscoting, wide porches, and cast-iron beds—but the imaginative food of chef Amanda Hallowell is reason enough to visit. Summertime North Haven regulars such as novelist Susan Minot and artist Eric Hopkins have come to sample her hyper-local dishes—a peppered-mackerel Caesar salad and a plate of sweet pickled beets, celery, and fennel, to name two. But you've also come to live out the pine-shaded, salty Maine fantasy: bike the island's 30 miles of roads, climb to the top of Ames Knob, laze on the beaches of Mullen's Head Park, or explore the art galleries on pint-size Main Street.

11 Mullins Lane; 207/867-2007; nebolodge.com. $

THE DAILY TO DO

Forecast:

☀ 62° SUNNY

high tide 5:45 pm | low tide 11:30 am

sunset 7:58 pm

THE OUTER CAPE CHORALE PRESENT:

21st Century Chorale Masterpieces

7 pm

TOWN HALL

☞ in the basket

Menu

bacon, tomato onion & spinach hash w/ poached egg

apricot granola yogurt parfaits

cherry & wild blueberry danish

PROVINCETOWN, MASSACHUSETTS

Salt House Inn

The Loft Suite at the Salt House Inn. Opposite: The chalkboard above the breakfast buffet.

The evening sky is Technicolor and the beaches quietly majestic. But when it comes to style, Provincetown comes up wanting, a Ye Old Looke built on nautical knickknacks and rainbow flags. Salt House Inn is an impeccably tailored relief. Opened last summer by partners David Bowd, an executive at André Balazs Hotels, and Kevin O'Shea, a former interior designer for Morgans Hotel Group, the 15-room inn is pared-down (whitewashed headboards; bentwood chairs; Edison bulbs) but feels true to its Cape Cod location. There's a claw-foot tub in the Loft Suite, for instance, and hanging over each bed is a canny assemblage of vintage tools and wooden signs. The service reflects the knowing but invisible hand of the contemporary innkeeper: a calligraphed blackboard offers the weather forecast each morning alongside a breakfast of pastries, egg burritos, and fresh-squeezed juice.

6 Conwell St.; 508/487-1911; salthouseinn.com. **$**

New York City

The Big Apple is undergoing yet another hotel building boom, with a wave of openings across the city, from leafy Greenwich Village to skyscraper-packed midtown. Historic refurbishments; glitzy towers; high-end boutique properties—here, our list of Manhattan's most exciting arrivals.

1 The Marlton

Hip hotelier Sean MacPherson's urbane inn has a rich literary past: Jack Kerouac and Lenny Bruce were once guests at the former Greenwich Village flophouse. Behind the original brick façade, weathered herringbone floors line a library filled with Beat novels, and the 107 diminutive rooms—most a snug 150 square feet—have ornate moldings and lighting fixtures that pay homage to the early-20th-century industrial designer Serge Mouille. Thoughtful details, such as products from Provençal perfumer Côté Bastide, complete the picture.

5 W. Eighth St.; 212/321-0100; marltonhotel.com. **$$**

A view of New York City from the Marlton's terrace.

Grape & Vine, the restaurant at Jade Hotel.

A suite at the High Line Hotel.

2 Jade Hotel

A 1920's-Paris sensibility defines this brick-clad Georgian-style building on a prime block in Greenwich Village. Inspired by legendary French designer Émile-Jacques Ruhlmann, the 113 rooms have Art Deco details (old-school rotary phones; clubby leather chairs) and vintage photos of pop icons such as the Rolling Stones. Art aficionados won't want to miss the dimly lit lobby lounge, which is stocked with a collection of design books curated by *Maker* magazine. For dinner, reserve one of the red velvet booths at the hotel's subterranean Grape & Vine restaurant and feast on cocoa-cinnamon-braised short ribs with mac and cheese.

52 W. 13th St.; 212/375-1300; thejadenyc.com. **$$**

3 High Line Hotel

Blink and you might mistake Chelsea's latest debut for an old-world university campus. Housed in a wing of the General Theological Seminary, which stands on a former apple orchard, the 1895 Gothic-style structure has stained-glass windows and cloistered courtyards that give it a stately, collegiate feel. But modernity isn't far away—hipster favorite Intelligentsia Coffee Bar opened its first East Coast shop in the mosaic-tiled lobby; cult bakery Mah Ze Dahr serves caramel-oatmeal bars from the hotel's 1963 Citroën van parked by the entrance; and it's just a short walk east to the High Line park.

180 10th Ave.; 212/929-3888; thehighlinehotel.com. **$$**

The nighttime view from the Refinery Hotel's rooftop bar and lounge.

4 Refinery Hotel

This 1912 edifice once housed hat factories on its top floors and a ladies-who-lunch tearoom in the lobby; now it's one of midtown's trendiest additions, thanks to Stonehill & Taylor, the architects behind the NoMad and Crosby Street hotels. The look? Distressed hardwood floors and 12-foot-high concrete ceilings; writing desks designed to resemble old sewing machine stands and factory-cart coffee tables. At dusk, the terrace draws fashionable Manhattanites with a cocktail menu conceived by a molecular biologist and former NASA consultant.

63 W. 38th St.; 646/ 664-0310; refineryhotel newyork.com. **$$$**

A Superior room at the Quin.

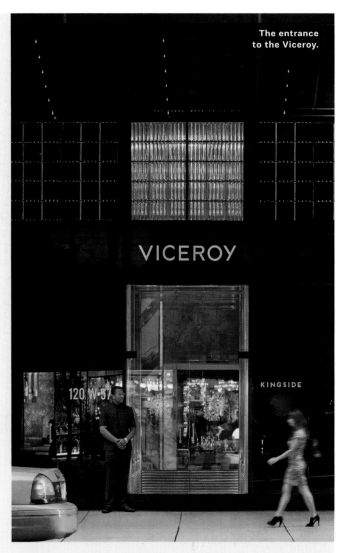

The entrance to the Viceroy.

VICEROY

120 W-57

KINGSIDE

5 The Quin

When you check in to the Quin, a stylish newcomer in Midtown West, you get much more than the key to an airy, 600-square-foot room. Fancy a private trunk show at Bergdorf Goodman or an after-hours tour of the Guggenheim? Personal travel attachés are on hand to curate bespoke experiences. Don't feel like leaving your custom Duxiana bed to change the music? Grab the bedside iPad mini, which you can also use to order room service or change the temperature settings. Bonus: the lobby-level art gallery showcases local talent such as graffiti artist Nick Walker and multimedia installations on a 14-foot video wall.

101 W. 57th St.; 212/245-7846; thequinhotel.com. **$$$$**

6 Viceroy

Style-conscious business travelers have a new stomping ground: the sleek, 29-story brick-and-glass Viceroy, the brand's Manhattan debut. On-site translators and high-tech wireless printing services are just a few of the office-away-from-home perks. Inside, a sophisticated retro design by heritage-chic specialists Roman & Williams—multipaned windows and brass hardware in the guest rooms; black-and-white tiles with scarlet grouting in the Kingside restaurant—sets the scene. If you're seeking refuge from the city, head to the rooftop bar and take in the bird's-eye view of Central Park.

120 W. 57th St.; 855/647-1619; viceroyhotelsandresorts.com. **$$$**

Bridgehampton's
Topping Rose House.

BRIDGEHAMPTON, NEW YORK

Topping Rose House

Between his Craft restaurants and his role as head judge on *Top Chef,* Tom Colicchio is one of the food world's biggest stars. Now he brings his culinary magic to an 1842 Greek Revival mansion in Bridgehampton, New York, with 22 rooms and cottages designed by Alexandra Champalimaud. The food, of course, takes center stage, and the locavore menu reinforces Colicchio's passion for fresh and sustainable ingredients. His inspiration? European country inns with restaurants: "It's all an extension of hospitality. We want this to be the place where once you're here, it's a warm embrace."

1 Bridgehampton–Sag Harbor Turnpike; 631/537-0870; toppingrosehouse.com. **$$$$**

Tom Colicchio prepares a dish in the kitchen. Above: A guest room.

MIDDLEBURG, VIRGINIA

Salamander Resort & Spa

Politicians and power players have long flocked to this lush region of stone-walled fields and grand estates in the heart of Virginia's burgeoning wine country. Ten years ago, sports and media tycoon Sheila Johnson purchased a 340-acre property here and began building Salamander Resort & Spa—a cosseting 168-room country house that opened in 2013. Despite its sprawling scale, the place feels surprisingly intimate; instead of a lobby, guests enter an elegant living room and wood-paneled library stocked with books and board games, while Johnson's own antiques and artwork, including a 14-foot-long tapestry once owned by Napoleon, are scattered throughout the property. The area has plenty of diversions—50 wineries within an hour's drive; a charming 18th-century village just down the road—but with two tennis courts, an indoor pool, and horses for trail riding, there's little reason to leave the grounds.

500 N. Pendleton St.; 866/938-7370; salamanderresort.com. **$$$**

An aerial view of the Salamander Resort & Spa.

The courtyard
at Zero George.

A grilled Cherry Point shrimp dish at Zero Café & Bar. Right: The hotel's drawing room.

CHARLESTON, SOUTH CAROLINA

Zero George

In a city known for antebellum-style inns and antiques-filled bed-and-breakfasts, a local iconoclast is shaking things up. Co-owners Dean Andrews and Lynn Easton—who ran the venerable Charleston Place hotel for 16 years—bring this genteel town its first truly contemporary retreat with Zero George, in the oak-lined Ansonborough district. The 18 guest rooms, spread out among five historic buildings (all circa 1800), have period pocket gardens and wide verandas; Farrow & Ball paint colors and Kravet linens make them look refreshingly up-to-date. Join a Lowcountry cooking class in the former kitchen house, which culminates with a Southern repast in a sunny courtyard flanked by azaleas and palms.

O George St.; 855/242-1864; zerogeorge.com. **$$**

A Signature Grande room with its candlelit terrace at the Gale South Beach & Regent Hotel.

Gale South Beach & Regent Hotel

If you're young, beautiful, and looking for value, you're likely staying at the Gale, a redo of a 1941 L. Murray Dixon hotel just a block from the ocean on Collins Avenue. It's no accident that the two entrances to the lobby shuttle you through either Dolce Italian, the two-tiered, boisterous restaurant that turns out house-made pasta al dente, or the *Mad Men*–evoking Regent Cocktail Club: it's all about the scene here. Amy Sacco's Rec Room, a lounge lined with old records, thumps in the basement, bringing out the South Beach party set to watch underground DJ's spin until sunrise. Fortunately, the 87 nautical rooms provide a serene respite from the din, with a white-and-navy-blue palette, 55-inch LED TV's, and large sea-facing balconies.

1690 Collins Ave.; 855/532-2212; galehotel.com. **$$**

A view of the shore from South Beach's James Royal Palm hotel.

A light-filled sitting area in one of the guest rooms. Left: The lobby coffee bar.

MIAMI

James Royal Palm

A retro vibe permeates the 393 rooms and public spaces in this Deco high-rise, the latest in a line of splashy Miami hotel openings, each one seemingly chicer than the last. The building's front façade is an exact replica of the 1939 Royal Palm resort; inside, you'll find terrazzo floors and porthole windows along with Midcentury-inspired furniture. Adding to the sense of authenticity is the Florida Cookery restaurant, an expansive open-air space that serves such locavore dishes as alligator empanadas and sorrel-lychee-glazed quail and oysters. Over-the-top pastimes abound, whether you're enjoying a healing salt soak at the spa or sipping Veuve Clicquot, chilled in a steel-and-glass champagne cooler in the superclub SL. How South Beach is that?

1545 Collins Ave.; 888/526-3778; jameshotels.com. **$$$$**

DALLAS

The Joule

A $78 million expansion overseen by hotel and restaurant designer Adam D. Tihany has added new polish to the Joule, in downtown Dallas. Originally a single 1927 neo-Gothic building, it has since expanded into three historic structures and now takes up nearly an entire city block, crowned with a cantilevered rooftop pool. Tihany's revamp includes 33 spacious rooms, suites, and penthouses—bringing the total to 160—an 8,000-square-foot Espa, and several boutiques. The transformation also debuted a sleek lobby bar (the brainchild of Los Angeles–based design group Team Over Six), which serves impeccably crafted cocktails. While the Dallas Museum of Art is a short walk away, there's no need to leave the hotel to see world-class art—owner Tim Headington's collection, with works by Andy Warhol and Richard Phillips, is showcased throughout the property.

1530 Main St.; 214/748-1300; thejouledallas.com. $$

united states+canada

35

Lake Austin
Spa Resort's
indoor pool.

AUSTIN, TEXAS

Lake Austin Spa Resort

A preternatural sense of calm reigns at the shorefront Lake Austin Spa Resort, facing a bluff at the edge of Texas Hill Country. Most guests come for the 25,000-square-foot limestone-and-cedar spa, renowned for its comprehensive treatment menu (traditional Thai floor massage, acupuncture, and aromatherapy, for example). Also on offer: meditation, healthy cooking, stand-up paddleboarding, and restorative yoga, as well as boat cruises and kayaking on Lake Austin. General manager for the past 16 years, Tracy York oversees the property and is a regular on the grounds, greeting guests by first name. "This place is designed to feel like your best friend's lake house," she says. Indeed, the resort is so welcoming some guests attend the nightly five-course dinners in their robes.

1705 S. Quinlan Park Rd.; 800/847-5637; lakeaustin.com. **$$$$**

Paddleboarding on Lake Austin. Above: Audubon prints in the living room.

21c Museum Hotel

Next door to Zaha Hadid's Contemporary Art Center Cincinnati is the second in a series of museum hotels conceived by Laura Lee Brown and Steve Wilson, a pair of Kentucky-based art collectors. As they did at outposts in Louisville, Kentucky, and Bentonville, Arkansas, the duo filled every nook and cranny with avant-garde pieces, from art channels in the Deborah Berke–designed guest rooms and interactive mirrored-glass pieces in the elevator cars to painting and sculpture exhibitions at Metropole restaurant. Our favorite detail: the solarium's color-shifting fiber-optic tapestries by Danish artist Astrid Krogh.

609 Walnut St.; 855/391-8726; 21cmuseumhotels.com. **$**

Yellow Penguin, a plastic sculpture by Cracking Art Group, and *OFF-SPRING: New Generation*, by Judy Fox, in the hotel's gallery. Opposite: The cocktail terrace.

The Langham
Chicago's
second-floor
lounge.

CHICAGO

The Langham

The city that helped pioneer Modernism now lays claim to the world's first—and only—hotel in a Ludwig Mies van der Rohe–designed building: the Langham, Chicago. Guests staying in the boxy, 1971 tower are welcomed into an airy ground-floor lobby that van der Rohe's grandson, architect Dirk Lohan, updated with classic Mies-inspired chairs and gold-beaded curtains. Double-height windows in the second-floor lounge allow for sweeping views of the Chicago River and city skyline. Upstairs, the 316 guest rooms are outfitted with travertine floors and bronze-edged headboards; glass walls in the bathrooms switch from transparent to opaque at the push of a button. David Rockwell is the brains behind the design of the Travelle restaurant, where chef Tim Graham taps in to his biochemistry background to elevate classic Mediterranean and Middle Eastern–inspired dishes. On the menu: inflated pita balloons with peppery *muhammara*, Moroccan pickled-feta lamb burgers, and *saganaki* chicken wings flamed at the table and extinguished with lemon juice. In this case, maybe more is more.

330 N. Wabash Ave.; 855/695-6664; langhamhotels.com. **$$$**

WHITEFISH, MONTANA

Lodge at Whitefish Lake

This both is and isn't your classic wilderness lodge. Yes, a full-size stuffed grizzly bear dominates the knotty alderwood lobby, moose and buffalo taxidermy stare down from the walls, and a floor-to-ceiling stone fireplace is lit year-round. But you'll also find decidedly un-rustic touches: some of the spacious suites have black granite kitchen countertops, as well as private balconies that look out onto the water. The ground-floor spa offers ginger body scrubs and volcanic-clay facials. And the hotel's Boat Lounge Club serves creative takes on local comfort food (think elk meatballs and halibut with couscous and braised fennel), prepared by chef Jeff Hobart. After a day spent hiking in nearby Glacier Park, watch the sun set over Monks Bay from the resort's tiki bar, preferably with a huckleberry spritzer in hand.

1380 Wisconsin Ave.; 877/887-4026; lodgeatwhitefishlake.com. $

The Lodge at
Whitefish Lake.
Opposite:
Dockside at
the hotel.

Hotel Jerome

This 125-year-old Aspen icon has a storied past: in the 1970's, Hunter S. Thompson was a regular at the hotel's J Bar; 19th-century silver miners used the property as a boardinghouse; and ghosts are said to haunt the place. Now a multimillion-dollar overhaul by Auberge Resorts has unveiled a shiny new chapter. While the Victorian red-brick façade remains, the common areas offer a playful take on the Old West: tufted leather sofas and mounted deer heads are juxtaposed with modern accents such as black-and-white cowhide rugs and crystal obelisks. The theme extends to the guest rooms, with cashmere curtains, plaid steamer-trunk dressers, and chairs upholstered in tartans and pinstripes. Add to all this the jaw-dropping mountain views and a lively après-ski scene, and Hotel Jerome is poised for another golden era.

330 E. Main St.; 800/331-7213; hoteljerome.com. **$$$$**

The lobby at
Hotel Jerome.

One of the bunk rooms at Outlook Lodge. Left: The outdoor fire pit.

Outlook Lodge

This converted rectory, now a handsome six-room inn, feels like an Eisenhower-era home. Set off a dirt road nearly 7,800 feet up in the Rocky Mountains, it has cone-shaped lamps and geometrically patterned rugs that compete for attention with mounted antlers, lacquered tree stumps, and pieces of contemporary art from owner Christian Keesee's personal collection. Settle in to your digs (the family suite has adult-length bunk beds, matching flat-screen TV's, and a cozy sunroom), then prepare a cup of steaming cocoa in the communal kitchen to drink by the lodge's fire pit.

6975 Howard St.; 855/463-2557; outlookgmf.com. **$**

45

The entrance to
the Ritz-Carlton,
Bachelor Gulch.

Ritz-Carlton, Bachelor Gulch

A storybook 12-floor lodge built into Beaver Creek Mountain, the newly revamped Ritz-Carlton cuts a commanding figure against a backdrop of aspens, pines, and powdery slopes. The hotel couldn't be better situated— mere steps from the chairlift, with a valet on hand to warm your boots and shuttle your skis to the snow. Stetson-wearing doormen usher guests into the cavernous Great Room, where clubby furnishings (distressed brown leather ottomans; striped earth-toned pillows) complement rough-hewn pine beams and a multistory fireplace of lichen-covered sandstone. The new Buffalos restaurant specializes in contemporary comfort food and Colorado craft beer, while an outpost of chef Wolfgang Puck's Spago turns out a hearty porterhouse steak for two. Achy muscles find relief at the Bachelor Gulch spa: a hot herbal poultice massage followed by a soak in the rock-lined grotto pool will have you ready for more backcountry runs come morning.

0130 Daybreak Ridge; 800/542-8680; ritzcarlton.com. **$$$$**

A king room at the Nobu Hotel at Caesars Palace.

Nobu Restaurant's take on bagels with lox. Below: Outside the hotel.

Nobu Hotel

Celebrity chef Nobu Matsuhisa can add *hotelier* to his résumé thanks to the opening of Nobu Hotel at Caesars Palace, in Las Vegas. Matsuhisa worked closely with architect David Rockwell to incorporate elements of his heritage throughout the property: upon arrival, you'll be treated to a cup of green tea and a traditional snack from the chef's hometown of Saitama, Japan. Most of the 181 suites and rooms have Japanese calligraphy on the walls and walk-in showers with black UMI tiles; hallways are lined with cherry-blossom-patterned carpets and origami-inspired lighting fixtures. Guests get first dibs on tables at the hotel's nearly 13,000-square-foot restaurant, though they can also order room service. For breakfast—a first for Matsuhisa— try the *kurobuta* sausage, *onsen* egg, and blueberry-and-*yuzu* soba pancakes.

3570 Las Vegas Blvd. S.; 800/727-4923; nobucaesarspalace.com. **$$**

Basecamp Hotel

Just minutes from both the water and Heavenly Mountain ski resort, Basecamp was designed with high-style adventurers in mind. Its 50 chic, sleepaway-camp-inspired rooms (some with bunk beds) substitute lanterns for lamps and survival guides for Gideon Bibles. For the ultimate stay, book the Great Indoors room, kitted out with a faux campfire, a forest-scene mural, and a canvas tent pitched over a king-size bed. Group meals, which vary by season (winter offerings include fondue and raclette), encourage hostel-like mingling—as do the outdoor fire pits, where you'll find guests sharing s'mores and trading stories about navigating the moguls at the nearby Gunbarrel run. Turn to the young, keyed-in staff for insider advice on where to go—with a little prodding they'll divulge secret locals-only spots, from wilderness lake hikes to the best places for untouched backcountry powder.

4143 Cedar Ave.; 530/208-0180; basecamphotels.com. **$$**

Colorful bric-a-brac in the lobby. Opposite: The Great Indoors room.

Brian Mock's sculpture made from tools and car parts inside S&R Lounge.

A king room at Hotel Zetta. Right: The Plinko wall in the lobby.

Hotel Zetta

For decades, San Francisco's Mid-Market neighborhood has been, to put it gently, a bit rough around the edges, a cross section of panhandlers and hustlers. But an influx of big-name restaurants and high-tech companies including Twitter and Foursquare have given the area new cachet. The latest addition? Viceroy Hotel Group's Hotel Zetta, a stylish business property catering to visiting movers and shakers. The interiors perfectly balance the contemporary (curved wooden walls above the beds) with the retro (artwork made of old floppy disks; chandeliers crafted from repurposed eyeglasses) and include up-to-the-minute amenities, such as Samsung Bluetooth-enabled smart TV's that allow you to stream content from mobile devices. There's also a slick cocktail lounge and a game room—shuffleboard, anyone?—and guests frequently settle the bar tab with a good-natured game of Plinko.

55 Fifth St.; 855/212-4187; hotelzetta.com. **$$**

The palm-tree-filled garden at El Encanto.

SANTA BARBARA, CALIFORNIA

El Encanto

Seven years and $134 million in the making, Orient-Express Hotels' takeover of the storied El Encanto (the brand's first West Coast resort) has reinvented a genteel slice of California history. The once quaint hillside hotel (a favorite of A-listers such as Clark Gable in the 1960's) has been reimagined to include 92 California Craftsman and Spanish-colonial-revival bungalows spread over seven lushly landscaped acres. Century-old charms were preserved (plantation-style shutters; wide patios) while luxe updates were added (mohair loveseats; pillows monogrammed with guests' initials). At the locally sourced restaurant, the bounty of vegetables and herbs from the on-site garden does not disappoint, nor does the aged white cheddar made with milk from the hotel's Holstein cow, Ellie.

800 Alvarado Place; 800/393-5315; elencanto.com. **$$$$**

Beverly Hills Hotel

Want to feel like a celebrity? Booking a room at Beverly Hills' legendary "pink palace" is a good place to start. If only these walls could talk—the 102-year-old hotel has hosted legions of personalities over the decades, from Elizabeth Taylor to Katy Perry. A recent face-lift has brightened the guest rooms and public spaces with walnut furnishings and a fresh palette (light cream, taupe, and silvery blues and greens). But not to worry—the hotel's signature red-carpet entrance and famous candy-colored exterior remain thoroughly intact. Come evening, crowds pack the star-studded Polo Lounge—where almost everyone orders the chopped McCarthy salad—and the balcony at Bar Nineteen12, to sip martinis until the wee hours.

9641 Sunset Blvd.; 800/276-2251; beverlyhillshotel.com. **$$$$**

A Presidential Suite vanity at the Beverly Hills Hotel. Opposite: The hotel's legendary pool.

A redwood-
clad Pool room
at the hotel.

The entrance
sign to the
Sparrows Hotel.
Right: The
hotel's pool and
restaurant.

PALM SPRINGS, CALIFORNIA

Sparrows Hotel

An antidote to Palm Springs' retro resorts, the Sparrows Hotel, set in a former 1950's motor lodge, emits a dude-ranch-in-the-desert vibe, with reclaimed-redwood walls and concrete floors. Consider it an Ace Hotel gone country: all 20 rooms have rustic furniture and vintage Swiss Army blankets; some come with horse-trough bathtubs. The restaurant, refashioned from a barn, loads its pizzas with organic peppers from the garden and pairs them with California wines. Despite a no-kids policy, youthful distractions abound—including a horseshoe pitch, splashy saltwater pool, and tennis court with old-timey wooden rackets.

1330 E. Palm Canyon Dr.; 760/327-2300; sparrowshotel.com. $

Sunshine Mountain Lodge

When it comes to the Rockies, travelers often overlook the Canadian wilderness in favor of the familiar peaks of Montana and Colorado, but the region's remoteness only adds to its seductive appeal. To reach this glass-and-wood lodge, you drive two hours from Calgary, park your car in Sunshine Village, leave your bag with a porter, and take a 17-minute gondola ride up 7,200 feet—but it's worth the trek. The only ski-in, ski-out hotel in Banff National Park, the area is a draw for nonskiers, too, thanks to a range of activities, from snowshoe-and-fondue treks with local guides to tobogganing, yoga, and movie nights in the game lounge. While each room emanates rustic mountain charm, the best are the two-story Premiere Loft suites, with stone fireplaces, jetted tubs, and remote-controlled shutters that open to reveal snowcapped bluffs.

1 Sunshine Village Access Rd.; 877/542-2633; sunshinemountainlodge.com. **$$**

**Slopeside at Sunshine
Mountain Lodge.**

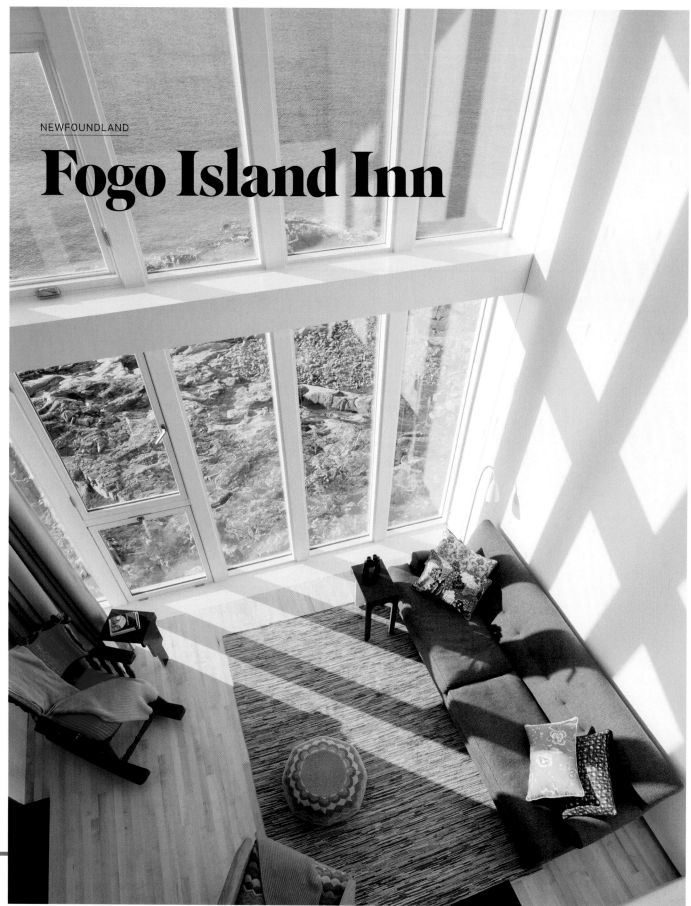

Fogo Island Inn

It's an incongruous sight: modern white boxes on stilts above the rocky, windswept coast of a small island off northeastern Newfoundland. But the 29-room Fogo Island Inn is actually infused with the area's DNA. It's the vision of Zita Cobb, a local fisherman's daughter turned tech entrepreneur, who launched an ambitious arts program on the island in 2006. For the new inn, Cobb tapped Newfoundland-born architect Todd Saunders, who also built four artists' studios, scattered across the island. The interiors were a collaboration between international designers (including the U.K.-based Ilse Crawford) and island craftspeople; quilters created bedspreads and other textiles, while boatmakers made furniture. Guests can learn about Fogo's icebergs and humpback whale population from experienced guides, and mingle with residents at the restaurant and art gallery. What's more, all profits go back to the community. In other words, it's a white box with soul.

Fogo Island; 709/658-3444; fogoislandinn.ca. **$$$$**

A view of Fogo Island Inn at sunset. Opposite: Overlooking a guest room lounge area.

The veranda at
Estancia La Bamba de
Areco, an hour's drive
outside Buenos Aires.

Caribbean
+Latin
America

One of the Cove
Eleuthera Resort &
Spa's two
private beaches.

ELEUTHERA, BAHAMAS

The Cove

Hidden on the two-mile-wide island of Eleuthera, the renovated Cove resort epitomizes barefoot luxury, with a simple white-on-white palette, locally built teak furnishings, and glassed-in patios. Soft-as-cashmere grass blankets the grounds and slopes gently down to two crescent swaths of pink sand where native *kamalame* trees are strung with hammocks, beckoning guests for afternoon naps and nighttime stargazing. Days are spent exploring the island's unspoiled surroundings, both overland and underwater, by jeep, bike, or snorkel (available for rent at the front desk). Every room here has easy beach access, but ocean lovers should book one of the 350-square-foot Caribbean Cove suites, just steps from the water.

Gregory Town; 888/776-9301; thecoveeleuthera.com. **$$**

A private deck
at Jakes Hotel.

Dining alfresco at Jakes. Below: A beachfront bungalow.

TREASURE BEACH, JAMAICA

Jakes Hotel, Villas, & Spa

If you're looking for a low-key Jamaican escape, Jakes is it. Everything exudes funky eccentricity, from the multiculti, hippie-chic décor to the Hoop Yogini classes (a mix of yoga and Hula-Hooping). The 43 stone bungalows—many right on the sand, others set atop rock outcrops that overlook the sea—were created by local theatrical designer Sally Henzell (expect bright yellow and blue stucco walls, pastel pillows and bedspreads, terra-cotta floors, and alfresco showers). Food is another highlight: two restaurants serve classic Jamaican dishes such as jerk chicken and pumpkin-and-ginger soup, and farm-to-table dinners are held monthly at communal tables under the mango trees. Or hop a fisherman's boat to Pelican Bar, a romantically ramshackle hut on a watery shoal 20 minutes away.

Calabash Bay; 877/526-2428; jakeshotel.com. **$**

One of Eden Roc's
two-bedroom
suites. Opposite:
A view of
Juanillo Beach.

PUNTA CANA, DOMINICAN REPUBLIC

Eden Roc

With its white Côte d'Azur–style buildings, Mediterranean restaurant,
and hushed European glamour, Eden Roc could easily be mistaken for
a resort on the French Riviera. Look closer, however, and this is pure
Caribbean—pristine beaches, lush jungle, and villas and suites done up
in tropical shades, accented with rich woods and fabrics. Every room
has a private terrace and plunge pool, with custom Italian furniture and
coral-and-stone bathtubs, courtesy of Milanese designers Carlo Belgir
and Marina Nova. It's the perfect place to spoil your little ones,
too, thanks to an enormous kids' club, complete with a video center,
play area, and even a mini-me spa.

Cap Cana; 809/469-7469; edenroccapcana.com. **$$$$**

The Livingston
Library at
Dorado Beach.

DORADO, PUERTO RICO

Dorado Beach, a Ritz–Carlton Reserve

In the 1950's, Laurance S. Rockefeller's 1,400-acre retreat on Puerto Rico's palm-fringed northern coast was a Caribbean hot spot for the Hollywood elite (Ava Gardner, John F. Kennedy, and Joan Crawford were regulars). Now a $342 million renovation has brought Dorado Beach back to its glory days. Private *embajadores* are at the ready to whisk guests in golf carts on jungle-lined paths to their two-story beachfront bungalows decorated with almond-colored fabrics and soothing sand-tinted walls. The colonial-style Su Casa villa has been meticulously restored (and can be all yours for a cool $25,000 a night). At the five-acre Spa Botánico, an unforgettable tree-house hammock massage will lull you into a blissful slumber. Adding to the wow factor is chef José Andrés's Puerto Rican–inspired Mi Casa restaurant, his first outpost in the Caribbean.

100 Dorado Beach Dr.; 800/241-3333; ritzcarlton.com. **$$$$$**

The lobby at Sugar Beach, a Viceroy Resort. Right: Beachfront dining.

ST. LUCIA

Sugar Beach, a Viceroy Resort

The 100-acre Jalousie Plantation, skirting a sleepy stretch of sand, was always lovely, its location, wedged between the towering Pitons—a UNESCO World Heritage site—second to none. But when British pub baron Roger Myers put $100 million into a rebranding by Viceroy, he raised the bar on an island already known for luxury. The result: 78 bleach-white accommodations including 42 hillside villas built with kiln-dried Central American hardwoods and filled with indigenous art; a tree-house spa made by a Rastafarian craftsman using 900-year-old Carib Indian techniques; and old-world staff uniforms (prim white cotton dresses for the housekeepers; top hats for the bellmen). The area's star attractions? Hundreds of triggerfish and clown shrimp that live in the nearby Anse de Pitons bay.

Soufrière; 800/235-4300; viceroyhotelsandresorts.com. **$$$$**

The Crane, on a cliff overlooking the Atlantic.

A guest room in the Crane's Residences by the Sea. Left: One of the suites' private pools.

Crane Residential Resort

The hum of whistling tree frogs signals your arrival at the Crane, the island's oldest continuously operating hotel. Cocooned from Barbados's buzzing Platinum Coast, the 40-acre resort sits high above a pink-sand beach in tiny St. Phillip. The two ways to get there: a glass-front elevator built into a precipice or 99 zigzagging stone steps. Cobblestoned pathways wind past pastel-hued clapboard cottages that house stylish boutiques, a gelato parlor, and a Japanese-and-Thai-inspired restaurant at the on-site village. A recent redo has added 252 sprawling suites, in addition to the Residences by the Sea, each with Italian marble floors, Oriental rugs, and up-to-the-minute tech amenities. The undeniable draw, though, is the placid turquoise sea, protected from the harsh waves of the east coast by an offshore reef.

St. Phillip; 886/978-5942; thecrane.com. **$$$$**

caribbean+latin america

Bequia Beach
Hotel's pool.

78

BEQUIA, THE GRENADINES

Bequia Beach Hotel

Part of a 32-island chain in the Grenadines, Bequia is blissfully sleepy:
the seven-square-mile speck has only 5,000 residents, a bucolic
whaling village, a few no-frills rum shacks, and just a handful of boutique
properties—the best of which is Bequia Beach Hotel. The 58 breezy
rooms (four-poster mahogany beds; rattan sofas) at this English-colonial-
style retreat open onto sun-drenched patios overlooking banana,
mango, and papaya trees. On Wednesday nights, you can devour grilled
seafood skewers with coconut and curry sauce at the hotel's beachside
restaurant Bagatelle while a traditional reggae band provides the
perfect West Indies soundtrack.

Friendship Bay; 784/458-1600; bequiabeach.com. $$

caribbean+latin america

Sunset at Flora
Farm, in San
José del Cabo.

Just-picked produce. Below: A private dining area.

LOS CABOS, MEXICO

Flora Farm

It isn't easy getting to Flora Farm—way out past the San José del Cabo marina, down a pothole-riddled road, and up a steep dirt lane. But once you arrive, you see what looks like a mirage amid the barren Mexican desert: 10 acres of organic herb and heirloom-vegetable gardens surrounding four rustic-chic guest cottages (white-splashed walls; handcrafted wood furniture; copper fixtures). Expat owners Patrick and Gloria Greene have quietly harvested the terrain for the past 17 years. The goal is to absorb the crowds from the year-old Flora's Field Kitchen, where dinner is booked months in advance by in-the-know travelers (chef Thomas Keller and George Clooney are fans). Outside, the Farm Bar pairs live music (a steady rotation of jazz, rock, and even flamenco) with inventive veggie-infused cocktails like the Carrot Farmanita; the couple also plan on unveiling an alfresco beer garden later this year.

San José del Cabo; 52-1624/355-4564; flora-farms.com. **$$$$**

The lobby at
the hacienda.

Hacienda San Angel

Colonial art and turn-of-the-century furnishings decorate this romantic 19-suite hideaway, tucked above the cobblestoned streets of Puerto Vallarta. The hotel has a series of interconnected villas—including one that was formerly owned by the actor Richard Burton, who gave it to his then wife, Susan Hunt, as a Valentine's gift—all built around multiple levels of gardens and terraces. While the seaside town offers many temptations, from colorful street markets to salsa dancing, you could easily spend an entire day just at the hacienda. Every corner reveals another treat, whether it's a frangipani-scented pool surrounded by angel sculptures, a mariachi band playing at the open-air restaurant, or a museum-quality collection of 18th-century artwork in Puerta del Cielo, the hotel's private chapel.

336 Miramar; 877/815-6594; haciendasanangel.com. **$$$**

Downtown México

The Revolution
Suite at the
Downtown México.
Opposite: The
hotel's rooftop bar
and terrace.

Star local hoteliers Grupo Habita have a knack for creating happening social hubs (case in point: New York's Hôtel Americano). Their fourth Mexico City hotel, in the former 17th-century Palacio de los Condes de Miravalle, is an oasis of style in the onetime Centro Histórico, the 500-year-old city center. The 17 guest rooms and public spaces, created by young Mexican architect duo Cherem-Serrano, blend original details, such as wood floors and fortress-thick brick walls, with tasteful handmade pine furnishings. In the atrium, a collection of artisanal Mexican boutiques sells everything from colorful scarves to mezcal. But you're really here for the rooftop scene, where jet-setters sip mango and tamarind margaritas near a sexy lap pool.

30 Isabel la Católica; 866/978-7020; downtownmexico.com. **$**

The main pool
at Mukul.

RIVAS, NICARAGUA

Mukul Beach, Golf & Spa

When Nicaraguan industrialist Carlos Pellas decided to build the country's first five-star hideaway, he chose an undeveloped stretch on the Pacific coast—a blank slate on which to create a new image for a country in flux. Pellas smartly added the familiar trappings of luxury: plunge pools; butlers; a spa with themed treatment rooms; a golf course designed by David McLay Kidd. Mukul soars on its strong sense of place: the staff is mostly local, and the furniture in the 23 cliffside *bohíos* and 12 freestanding beach villas is built by hand (unique touches include headboards made of rum-barrel staves and polished pewter tables). Grass-fed Nicaraguan beef, as well as Pellas's own excellent rum, Flor de Caña, is served at the beachfront restaurant. Most of all, there is a palpable feeling of pride in a place destined to help transform this under-the-radar retreat into Central America's next fashionable destination.

Guacalito de la Isla; 505/2563-7100; mukulresort.com. **$$$$**

Native parrots
on the balcony of
the Nayara Suite.

ARENAL NATIONAL PARK, COSTA RICA

Nayara Hotel, Spa, & Gardens

In a country known for its natural wonders, the 3,740-foot Arenal Volcano is arguably the centerpiece. Though the volcano is now dormant, travelers still flock to this region for wildlife spotting, white-water rafting, and kayaking on Lake Arenal. Make your base the revamped Nayara Hotel, Spa & Gardens, where the 50 wooden casitas are outfitted with plantation furniture and open onto wide decks with jaw-dropping volcano views. After exploring the area's lava fields and rain forests, pamper yourself with a mud bath at the hotel spa or a wine tasting on the terrace bar—or simply relax by the pool, whose graceful curves mirror the shape of the volcano.

La Fortuna de San Carlos; 866/311-1197; arenalnayara.com. **$ $**

PUNTARENAS, COSTA RICA

Kura Design Villas

The northwestern province of Guanacaste has always been the site of Costa Rica's splashiest hotels—but all eyes are moving south to the lesser-known province of Puntarenas. A bumpy, 20-minute drive up a steep mountain from the tiny town of Uvita leads to the sleek Kura Design Villas, the first property of its kind to open in the region. Set within a rain forest and overlooking jungle-lined beaches, the hotel is the passion project of a local couple (he's the architect; she's a marine biologist) who partnered with sustainable-hospitality group Cayuga Collection. The six airy, solar-powered guest rooms come with glass-walled rain showers and bamboo ceilings. At the heart of the property is the saltwater infinity pool, and it's no accident it faces west. Come sunset, order a refreshing Guaria Morada cocktail, made with sugarcane liquor, blackberries, and coconut cream, and settle into a white leather chaise for the colorful show.

Uvita de Osa; 506/8521-3407; kuracostarica.com. **$$$$**

The lobby at
Sofitel Legend
Santa Clara.

CARTAGENA, COLOMBIA

Sofitel Legend Santa Clara

If there's a turning point in the story of modern Cartagena, it's 1995, when Sofitel opened the luxe Santa Clara, carved from the shell of a 17th-century convent in the quiet San Diego neighborhood. On the heels of an extensive three-year renovation, the hotel is back in the limelight. The 17 colonial-style suites, with their high ceilings, walk-in closets, and handloomed curtains, are now grand enough to host heads of state; some of the other 105 spacious rooms have sweeping views of the sea. And with the recent opening of the French-inspired 1621 Restaurant— try the *mondongo* tripe soup—the city's already impressive dining scene has reached new heights.

39-29 Calle del Torno; 800/763-4835; sofitel.com. **$$$$**

JW Marriott

Just two blocks from the Plaza de Armas, this opulent hotel should be a mandatory stop for international travelers en route to Machu Picchu or the Sacred Valley. After a seven-year restoration, the 16th-century former convent now has 153 spacious guest rooms, awash in muted browns and tans and enriched with oxygen for dealing with Cuzco's high altitude. Charming Spanish-colonial touches such as stone colonnades and flagstone patios fill the property. The showstopper? A glimmering sun sculpture in the lobby (inspired by Incan iconography) crafted from 65,000 Swarovski crystals.

432 Calle Ruinas; 800/228-9290; marriott.com. **$$**

Qespi Bar, at the
JW Marriott Cusco.
Opposite: The
hotel at nightfall.

An Atelier room
on the second
floor at Hotel B.

LIMA, PERU

Hotel B

With contemporary galleries and a boho-chic vibe, Lima's seaside Barranco neighborhood is fast emerging as the city's cultural hub. It's a fitting location for Hotel B, the Belle Époque former residence of the aristocratic García Bedoya family. A meticulous two-year restoration by Peruvian architect David Mutal and interior designers Jordi Puig and Sandra Masías revived the original marble floors and exposed wooden beams, while additions like a jasmine-fringed rooftop terrace, with its sexy cocktail bar, provide a dose of 21st-century glamour. Head to Lucía de la Puente's modern art gallery, then walk through a passageway to dine at the hotel's seafood tapas spot, where local chef-of-the-moment Oscar Velarde plays with Mediterranean flavors.

301 San Martín; 51-1/206-0800; hotelb.pe. **$$$**

Casa Mosquito's library and lounge.

Steps leading to the hotel. Right: The Heitor Villa-Lobos Suite.

IPANEMA, BRAZIL

Casa Mosquito

It's not often we discover an impeccably styled, discreet gem in the center of sprawling Rio, but Casa Mosquito is just that. Created by French expats Benjamin Cano and Louis Planès, the five guest rooms—each named after a famous Carioca artist—are decorated with vintage Brazilian furnishings, tropical-print curtains, and hand-cut-mosaic-tile showers, all sourced from local flea markets and shops. This spring, the duo will unveil a modern annex to the original 1948 house, bringing the total room count to 10 and incorporating a pool and a bar that serves killer tropical caipirinhas. An ideal location, just a stone's throw from the mythic Copacabana and Ipanema beaches, completes the picture.

Rua Saint Roman; 55-21/3586-5042; casamosquito.com. **$$**

VALE DOS MELLOS, BRAZIL

Botanique Hotel & Spa

High in the mountains of Vale dos Mellos, 160 miles northwest of São Paulo, sits a stone-and-glass lodge conceived to showcase the best of the country. There's the wine cellar (all Brazilian bottles), the food (farm-to-fork), and the furnishings (sourced by Adélia Borges, the country's leading design authority). The six suites and 11 villas are built with reclaimed wood and have terraces that overlook the valley. This is not luxury to satisfy all tastes—the wooden beams are over a century old, the bathrooms doorless, and the décor on the spare side. Still, the range of activities—horseback riding, cooking classes, even capoeira— is enough to please the most discriminating guests.

Campos do Jordão; 55-12/3797-6877; botanique.com.br. **$$$$**

The hotel's restaurant, Mina, overlooking the Mantiqueira Mountains. Opposite: Guests admiring the view.

Casa Chic's pool,
with a view of
Río de la Plata.

CARMELO, URUGUAY

Casa Chic

With its pastoral surroundings, boutique wineries, and farm-to-table dining, Uruguay's Carmelo region has long been a go-to weekend getaway for stylish Argentines. The latest property to raise the cool quotient: Casa Chic, a 20-room inn set on 250 acres of untouched forest. Owned by Federico Bonomi, the fashion genius behind Buenos Aires–based brands Kosiuko and Herencia, it has eclectically decorated rooms (plush dome chairs; rough-hewn wooden tables), sleek all-white bathrooms, and a showstopping pool on the edge of Río de la Plata. For local wine tastings, head 20 minutes north to Finca Narbana, a restored turn-of-the-century farmhouse and winery that produces Tannats and Viogniers.

Calle Límite Colonia Belgrano y Km 1 del Río de la Plata; 598-540/4030-3334; casa-chic.com. **$$**

Buenos Aires

An innovative spirit has taken hold in and around Argentina's capital. Forward-thinking hoteliers are energizing the city with new and reimagined boutique projects, tapping into its vibrant culture and colorful history for inspiration. The result? Distinctive properties that showcase authentic Argentinean character with a sophisticated edge.

1 Estancia La Bamba de Areco

Criollo horses. Century-old cattle ranches. Argentina's grassy Pampas is at its most seductive at this renovated 19th-century ranch just west of Buenos Aires. The 11 guest rooms—each with canopied beds and antique furnishings—are named after a resident pony, while the former carriage house is now a lounge with photographs of cowboy life. That clomping you hear throughout the property? The hotel's professional polo team, likely in the thick of a match.

2760 San Antonio de Areco; 54-11/4519-4996; labambadeareco.com.
$$$$

Horseback riding on the grounds of Estancia La Bamba.

The exterior of the Hotel Boca Juniors.

The suite at Hotel Pulitzer.

2 Hotel Boca Juniors

A mural by young Argentine star Diego Maradona greets you in his namesake suite at the world's first soccer-themed hotel, which pays homage to Buenos Aires's much-adored club, Boca Juniors. Uruguayan architect Carlos Ott is responsible for the design, in which convex glass walls allow sunlight to flood the ample rooms. The hotel is a *fútbol* fanatic's nirvana: a museum displays vintage memorabilia (classic photos; old-school cleats), rooms are stocked with historic soccer documentaries, and, on certain nights, you may even bump into a player—the top floors are reserved for the team before game days.

243 Tacuari; 54-11/4590-8540; hotelbocajuniors.com. **$$**

3 Hotel Pulitzer

Fashion designer Lázaro Rosa-Violán brings avant-garde charm to this hotel, in a city full of historical restoration projects. Hidden in tango hotbed Microcentro, the 104-room Pulitzer has chicly nautical interiors— think steel-trimmed modular furniture, navy mosaicked showers, and round mirrors. In winter, forage through the impressive collection of art books in the library, or dive into the culture scene at the nearby National Museum of Fine Arts; come summer, join bronzed guests clad in designer swimwear at the terrace pool, where B.A.'s cityscape unfurls under a glowing South American sun.

907 Calle Maipú; 54-11/4316-0800; hotelpulitzer.com. **$$**

A seating area in the hotel's Ambassador Suite.

4 Four Seasons

Fresh off a $40 million revamp, this Buenos Aires landmark occupies both a modern 12-story tower and a handsome 1920's mansion, connected by immaculately landscaped gardens. The décor reflects the era of each building: the 158 main rooms are bright and airy, with splashes of color (fresh orchids and roses), texture (mahogany furnishings), and sheen (Italian-marble bathrooms), and the seven sprawling Mansion suites embody classic French opulence (toile de Jouy wallpaper; antique tea sets). Don't miss dinner at the hotel's Nuestro Secreto restaurant, when locals fill the courtyard for asado-style meats and live jazz.

1086 Calle Posadas; 800/332-3442; fourseasons.com. **$$$$**

Hub Porteño's restaurant courtyard.

The stone façade at Hotel Club Francés.

5 Hub Porteño

The allure of this gem in the Recoleta area is its impressive ability to unlock the best Buenos Aires has to offer. Whether you're an aspiring polo player looking to meet a team member, or an architecture buff eager for a city tour with a noted interior designer, almost anything is within reach, thanks to the little black book of the Hub's well-connected owner, Gonzalo Robredo. The intimate hotel has 11 light-filled suites, with Belle Époque furnishings and paintings from the celebrated art collection of the late Amalia Lacroze de Fortabat; no surprise—she was a family friend.

1967 Rodríguez Peña; 54-11/4815-6100; hubporteno.com. **$$$**

6 Hotel Club Francés

Since opening in 1866, the storied Club Francés has drawn generations of politicians and writers to the genteel Recoleta neighborhood. While the city's intelligentsia still congregates at the lobby bar, the upper level was recently turned into a 28-room hotel filled with period furniture. A grand marble staircase leads to luminous parlors adorned with large chandeliers and 20th-century oil paintings; the rooms have deep beds with recycled-wood headboards and plush armchairs. Bonus: the city's high-end shopping corridor is just beyond the front door.

1832 Rodríguez Peña; 54-11/4812-5235; hotelclubfrances.com.ar. **$$**

The infinity
pool at the Vines
Resort & Spa.

UCO VALLEY, ARGENTINA

Vines Resort & Spa

Who doesn't harbor a fantasy of owning a villa in a wine region, walking amid the vines in the morning, and, come afternoon, swimming in a private lake? You can realize that dream—without the price tag—at the Vines Resort & Spa, in Mendoza's burgeoning Uco Valley. Every evening, guests are encouraged to gather around a long communal table hewn from old wine barrels to sample one of the estate's boutique old-vine blends (it produces 18 varietals). At the hotel's Siete Fuegos restaurant, chef Francis Mallmann, Argentina's version of Thomas Keller, serves rustic, open-flame specialties such as goat prepared on heated stones with rosemary and *jarilla*. After dinner, unwind in one of 22 spacious villas, decorated with locally made crafts such as handwoven rugs and blankets—symbols of the property's commitment to supporting Argentinean artistry.

Tunuyán; 54-261/676-4300; vinesresortandspa.com. **$$$$**

The resort's vineyards, with the Andes in the distance. Above: Grilled peaches with whipped cream at Siete Fuegos.

Sun-drenched
vineyards at
Casa de Uco.

UCO VALLEY, ARGENTINA

Casa de Uco

Set in the Andean foothills, where the sun shines 330 days a year, Casa de Uco is best reached by helicopter—the ideal way to appreciate the resort's thoughtful integration within the greater landscape. The 16 spacious suites (which will soon be joined by 10 two-bedroom bungalows), made of native stone, guarantee a view of the estate's Petit Verdot, Torrontés, and Malbec vines. The hotel is geared toward wine aficionados seeking deeper immersion in the region's viticulture, with activities that range from intimate tastings in the estate's subterranean grotto to horseback rides and hands-on blending sessions with renowned resident winemaker Alberto Antonini.

Tunuyán; 54-115/245-5550; casadeuco.com. **$$$$**

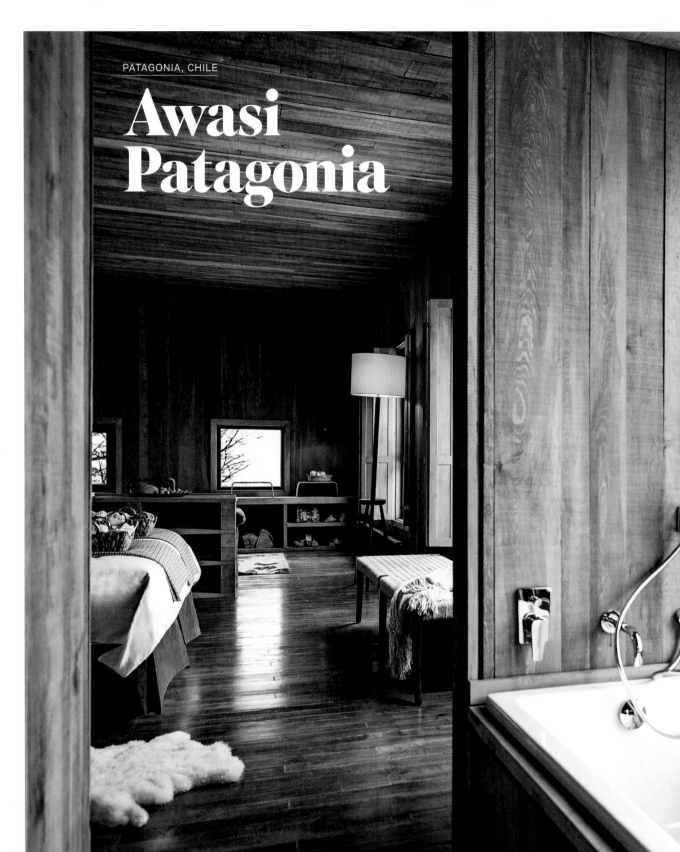

Awasi Patagonia

Inside one of Awasi's villas, built from native *lenga* wood. Opposite: A villa exterior.

Chile's southern province of Última Esperanza, which poetically translates as "last hope," is a sparsely populated realm—men on horseback still drive cattle along the roads and condors perch on sandstone sierras. But Awasi Patagonia makes the end of the earth feel more like home. Designed by noted Chilean architect Felipe Assadi, the lodge's 12 contemporary villas are constructed from indigenous *lenga* wood, each with a stone fireplace, sheepskin rugs, and an oversize hot tub overlooking the Torres del Paine mountains. After a guided trek through the neighboring Pampas, join gauchos from Awasi's estancia for an asado meal at the lodge's rustic restaurant.

4 Tocopilla, Torres del Paine; 888/880-3219; awasi.cl; all-inclusive; three-night minimum. **$$$$$**

Refugia Lodge

Chile's largest archipelago, known for its wildflower fields, picture-perfect rocky beaches, and centuries-old wooden churches, has just welcomed the unlikeliest of architectural monuments: Refugia. The contemporary retreat is sheathed in wood and hovers above a glass-and-concrete base. Twelve guest rooms clad in native *mañío* wood command unobstructed vistas of the salmon fishermen tracing the tide, while downstairs, the crackling of a roaring fireplace fills the austere lounge. If quietly sipping Carménère while counting the shades of gray shifting across the inland sea fails to quicken the pulse, an outing to the dramatic fjords and tiny fishing villages is just a custom-kitted boat ride away.

217 San José Playa Castro; 56-65/772-080; refugia.cl. **$$$$**

Refugia Lodge
at dusk.

Behind the bar
at Lime Wood,
in Hampshire,
England.

Europe

The Amalia Rodrigues Room at Casa Amora, near the Príncipe Real.

Breakfast in the lounge area. Below: The living room of the Duplex Suite.

LISBON

Casa Amora

Lisbon has its fair share of charming B&B's, but Casa Amora is the city's most sophisticated newcomer. A former residence dating back to 1907, the antiques-filled guesthouse, with a multicolored tile façade and mansard roof, feels like a home away from home. Book one of four Studio rooms, each with its own kitchen and sitting area. Private entrances lead to either the Amoreiras Garden or the Alto São Francisco stairs, which are lined with old streetlamps and bougainvillea. In the morning, don't miss a breakfast of Spanish *tortilla* and fruit clafouti, served in the inner courtyard patio, overlooking the vertical garden.

13 Rua de João Penha; 351/919-300-317; casaamora.com. $

SEVILLE, SPAIN

Hotel Alfonso XIII

Built in 1929 to host foreign dignitaries, Seville's Hotel Alfonso XIII has never abdicated its role as the city's premier address for discerning travelers. But even royal retreats need an occasional overhaul, which is why Starwood spent nine months and $25 million restoring the landmark—an Andalusian architectural confection of colorful tiles, carved plaster, and curlicue ironwork. Traditionalists may grieve over the disappearance of ornate furnishings from the 151 guest rooms and suites, but we love the lighter colors, checkerboard marble floors, and sexy shimmer of vivid silks.

2 San Fernando; 800/325-3589; hotel-alfonsoxiii-seville.com. **$$**

A view of
Hotel Alfonso XIII
at nightfall.

121

El Lodge

High in the Sierra Nevada, this Nordic-inspired hotel resembles a cozy log cabin, but you're far from the backwoods here—a point clearly telegraphed at the entrance, where EL LODGE is playfully spelled out in giant showbiz-style lights. The Andrew Martin–designed interior is all blond wood and faux-hide upholstery, with an elegant restaurant serving local game and organic caviar. Rooms and suites have walls of solid Finnish pine and such quirky design details as antler chandeliers and dressers crafted from repurposed suitcases. There's also an alfresco heated pool and small spa, but most guests make a beeline for the tabletop fire pits, surrounded by low-slung loungers.

8 Calle Maribel; 34/95-848-0600; ellodge.com. **$$$**

The patio, overlooking the slopes. Opposite: A Deluxe double room at El Lodge.

Domaine de
la Baume's
formal gardens.

Domaine de la Baume

French hotelier and tastemaker Jocelyne Sibuet's latest project proves that earthiness and elegance aren't mutually exclusive. The 99-acre estate evokes a Provençal fantasy, from the 18th-century villa's façade (ocher-hued with sky-blue shutters) to the undulating landscape of olive groves and a stone pool framed by plane trees. The eight guest rooms, with their toile de Jouy headboards, woodblock-print curtains, and walls painted in rich colors, draw inspiration from the East India Company, which imported fabrics through nearby Marseilles in the 1600's. Beyond the hotel gates lies the postcard-perfect village of Tourtour, with its narrow cobblestoned streets and flower-filled town square.

2071 Rte. d'Aups; 33-4/57-74-74-74; domaine-delabaume.com. **$$$$**

Altapura's
lounge and
iron fireplace.

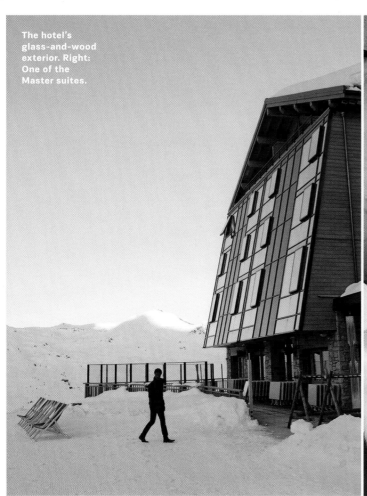

The hotel's glass-and-wood exterior. Right: One of the Master suites.

VAL THORENS, FRANCE

Altapura

Hidden in the Vallée des Belleville at an elevation of 7,545 feet, Europe's highest hotel exudes après-ski opulence. Scandinavian-style interiors incorporate light-colored wood draped in white faux fur and backlit screens with snowflake cutouts. There's no shortage of creature comforts, thanks to a 10,000-square-foot spa with a stone tepidarium, seven treatment rooms lined with birch branches, and an ice "igloo" where guests exfoliate their skin using snow. At the hotel's La Laiterie restaurant, hearty fondues are made from regional cheeses and wines. Order a pot of the Chablais blend and take in the view of Les Trois Vallées' six glaciers.

Rue du Soleil; 33-4/80-36-80-36; altapura.fr. **$$$**

europe

Café Royal

**Pastries on display
at Café Royal.
Opposite: Outside
the hotel, on
Regent Street.**

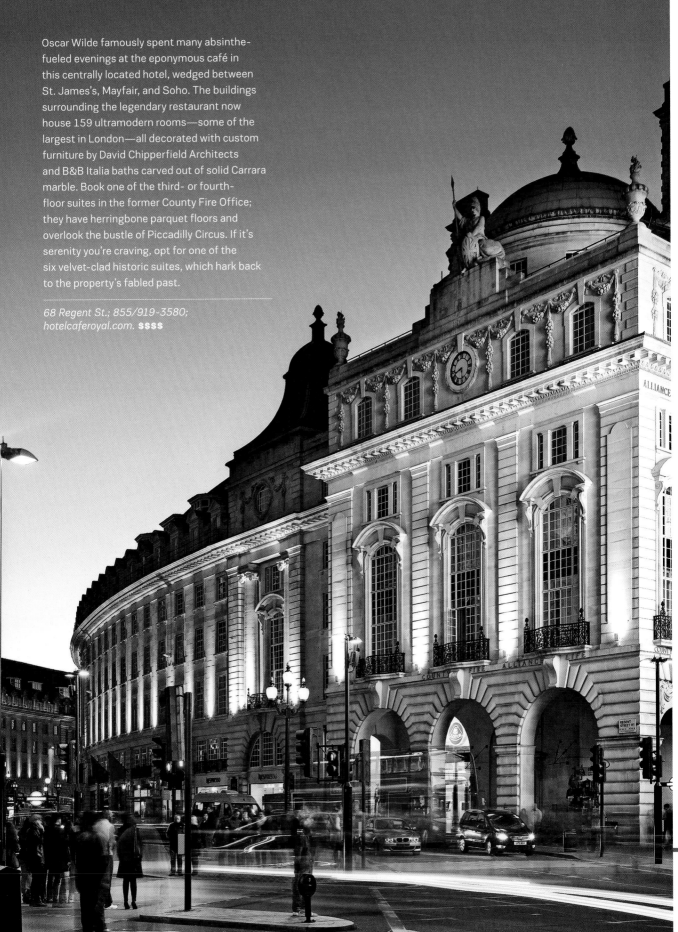

Oscar Wilde famously spent many absinthe-fueled evenings at the eponymous café in this centrally located hotel, wedged between St. James's, Mayfair, and Soho. The buildings surrounding the legendary restaurant now house 159 ultramodern rooms—some of the largest in London—all decorated with custom furniture by David Chipperfield Architects and B&B Italia baths carved out of solid Carrara marble. Book one of the third- or fourth-floor suites in the former County Fire Office; they have herringbone parquet floors and overlook the bustle of Piccadilly Circus. If it's serenity you're craving, opt for one of the six velvet-clad historic suites, which hark back to the property's fabled past.

68 Regent St.; 855/919-3580; hotelcaferoyal.com. **$$$$**

English Country Inns

The British may not have invented the concept of the countryside inn, but they essentially perfected it. In the sylvan expanses of the New Forest, the winding alleys of Southampton, and the sheep-dotted nooks and crannies of the Cotswolds, you'll find a smattering of rural properties that exude a profound sense of place.

1 Barnsley House

Former resident Rosemary Verey's legendary Arts and Crafts–style gardens surround this decade-old, 18-room hotel, still the Cotswolds' most stylish place to stay. The best rooms are scattered across two upper stories of the main house, with its labyrinth of hallways. Room 1 is the standout, a light-flooded study in milky whites and grays; the spacious bathroom has his-and-hers tubs. Mullioned windows provide three exposures over the gardens, while cozy window seats might as well come with a Nick Drake soundtrack.

Barnsley, Cirencester; 44-12/8574-0000; barnsleyhouse.com. **$$$**

The patio and gardens outside Barnsley House.

The restaurant at Lime Wood, in the New Forest.

2 Pig in the Wall

The team behind the Pig—a food-focused hideaway in Hampshire's New Forest—has done it again. The Pig in the Wall brings its older sibling's rural charms to Southampton—ideal for guests who prefer cobblestoned streets to woodland walks. Here, a dozen rooms are built into the city's medieval walls and packed with eccentric flourishes, from mismatched furnishings to leather-bound radios. And while the property is too small for a proper restaurant, it maintains plenty of foodie appeal: a deli counter offers "piggy bites" such as coppa with pickled carrots, while in-room larders are stocked with Serious Pig salami.

Western Esplanade, Southampton; 44-23/8063-6900; thepighotel.com. **$**

3 Lime Wood

Eighty miles southwest of London, the New Forest was developed in 1079 by William the Conqueror, who used it as his private hunting ground. At its green heart now stands Lime Wood, a 29-room hotel surrounded by reflecting pools, swings dangling from oak trees, and wacky animal lawn sculptures (bronze jackrabbits and sheep). On soggy days, guests borrow playful pink polka-dot wellies from the mudroom and tromp through the woods searching for wild ponies and deer, then retreat to the Regency manor house to curl up on moss-hued velvet French chairs by the wood-burning fireplace.

Lyndhurst; 44-23/8028-7177; limewoodhotel.co.uk. **$$$**

The library at
Ett Hem, in
the Lärkstan
district.

STOCKHOLM

Ett Hem

This may well be the year of hotel-as-home, and the 12-room Ett Hem, in Stockholm's residential Lärkstan district, is a prime example. Interiors by London-based Ilse Crawford, who was also behind Soho House London and New York, mix Midcentury Scandinavian furniture with custom-made brass cocktail cabinets, Gotland sheepskins, and contemporary art from the owner's personal collection. Go ahead, roam the house: play the piano in the bright living room, pull a novel off a shelf, or sneak down to the kitchen for a midnight snack. We especially appreciated how every member of the staff, from the chef to the housekeeper, stopped to offer us a warm *välkommen*.

2 Sköldungagatan; 877/234-7033; slh.com. **$$$$**

BERLIN

Das Stue

The indoor lap pool at
Das Stue, in Berlin's
Embassy Quarter.
Opposite: The hotel's
first-floor lounge.

On leafy Drakestrasse—between the Tiergarten park and the city's zoo—this 80-room retreat has quietly stolen the spotlight in Berlin. Housed in the former Danish embassy, Das Stue derives its name from the Danish word for "living room," a concept that interior designer Patricia Urquiola has embraced to tasteful effect, seamlessly combining a 1939 Neoclassical building with a new five-story addition. Homey but stylish touches, such as Horst photographs and library nooks with shag rugs, enchanted us. Request a room in the new wing for a view of the zoo's ostriches and gazelles; you'll get a glimpse of the same scene while enjoying the lavish breakfast in the dining room downstairs.

1 Drakestrasse; 49-30/311-7220; das-stue.com. **$$**

The Waldorf Astoria Berlin's modern exterior. Left: Mixing a drink at the Lang Bar.

BERLIN

Waldorf Astoria

The floor-to-ceiling windows provide an unfiltered and entirely dramatic view of the city: here is Berlin, in all its gritty, peculiar glory. The Waldorf Astoria tower, 32 stories tall, anchors the reviving City West neighborhood around the Tiergarten, where history (the preserved ruins of the Kaiser Wilhelm Church) rubs elbows with the future (the new Helmut Newton museum), and the city's creative energy is palpable. The 232 well-appointed rooms are inviting and luxurious, with soft beige, brown, and gold finishes. Among the many welcome amenities is a Nespresso machine (which really ought to be standard issue in every hotel room from now on). While the lobby may carry a tinge of the corporate, the Lang Bar is dark and moody and just what you will want at the end of the day.

28 Hardenbergstrasse; 800/445-8667; waldorfastoria.com. **$$**

VERBIER, SWITZERLAND

W

The mountain village of Verbier has long attracted European royalty and Hollywood glitterati for its blue skies, undulating pistes, renowned après-ski scene, and summer music festival. The newest hangout is the W brand's first Alpine property. Interiors may be retro-cool and funky (globe lights; furry pillows; cowhide chairs), but the hotel's Arola restaurant, run by celebrated Spanish chef Sergi Arola, is serious business: expect innovative tapas such as oxtail ravioli with foie gras and Iberian-pork carpaccio. After dark, the party heads belowground to Carve, where DJ's unleash a high-altitude—and high-octane—dance party.

70 Rue de Médran; 877/946-8357; whotels.com. **$$$$**

A guest room
at the W Verbier.

The Panorama Suite
at Alpina Gstaad.

Alpina

With the arrival of the Alpina, the first luxury hotel to be built in Gstaad in a century, Switzerland's elite wintertime playground finally has a contemporary clubhouse to call its own. Better known for its deep-pocketed regulars than for its cool cachet, Gstaad has long lacked what the Alpina delivers: a cosmopolitan vibe and youthful sensibility—complete with an outpost of the Japanese restaurant Megu, a cutting-edge art collection, and a lounge destined to become the ultimate meeting spot for area scenesters. The Six Senses Spa, with its curving cream walls, may feel a bit out of keeping with the rest of the property's warm embossed leathers, herringbone wools, and antique fir accents, but the soothing hot-stone massage more than makes up for any aesthetic misstep.

23 Alpinastrasse; 41-33/888-9888; thealpinagstaad.ch. **$$$$**

europe

Aman Canal Grande

The Aman Canal Grande. Opposite: A corner table in the Yellow Dining Room.

In a city whose reputation was built on extravagant displays of wealth, and whose beauty today is more of a crumbling, decadent sort, the Aman resort is a curiously austere space set within the 16th-century Palazzo Papadopoli. A tasteful merger of 21st-century design and neo-Renaissance and Rococo splendor, the public salons and 24 suites were refurbished in an 18-month renovation requiring an average of 100 artisans on site daily. Elaborate plasterwork, original Murano chandeliers, and freshly abluted gilt contrast with angular, contemporary furniture in gunite gray, studio white, and other muted shades. Despite the new minimalism, old-world treasures appear at every turn, including an original fresco by Giovanni Battista Tiepolo crowning a dining room that's covered in vermilion damask.

1364 Calle Tiepolo, San Polo; 800/477-9180; amanresorts.com. **$$$$$**

Hotel Monteverdi's
infinity pool.

The hotel's La Pieve Suite. Right: A stone pathway through the property's grounds.

VAL D'ORCIA, ITALY

Hotel Monteverdi

Cobblestoned paths, lavender-scented gardens, and an idyllic pool make Monteverdi the medieval hilltop escape you've been waiting for. With just 10 suites, the scale is decidedly intimate. Stylish farmhouse interiors are by Roman designer Ilaria Miani: all neutral hues, rich textures, and whitewashed antique wood. Of course, you also have the picturesque setting, in the tiniest of villages (population: 25), on one of the highest hills in the Val d'Orcia, recognized by UNESCO to be among the region's most beautiful valleys. And thanks to a restoration by the owners— an Italian-American family who have taken a slow-and-steady approach to integrating the property into the town—it's the kind of getaway that encourages hunkering down, even though the best of Tuscan wine- and-food country is just a short drive away.

Castiglioncello del Trinoro; 866/644-0787; monteverdituscany.com. **$$$**

europe

143

Rome

The Eternal City is a contrast of medieval wonders and cosmopolitan style, and nowhere is this mix more clearly on display than in Rome's newest crop of hotels. Well-worn façades concealing high-design interiors; centuries-long histories that underscore a building's many lives and layers; extravagant, of-the-moment comforts and amenities—you'll find it all here.

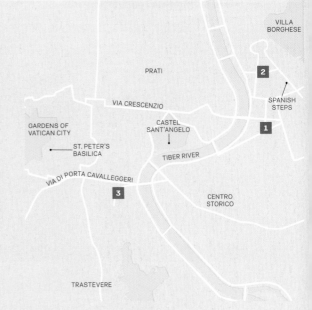

VILLA BORGHESE

PRATI

VIA CRESCENZIO

SPANISH STEPS

2

GARDENS OF VATICAN CITY

CASTEL SANT'ANGELO

ST. PETER'S BASILICA

1

TIBER RIVER

VIA DI PORTA CAVALLEGGERI

CENTRO STORICO

3

TRASTEVERE

1 J.K. Place Roma

The team behind the chic J.K. Place hotels in Capri and Florence has brought its deft blend of high style and genuine warmth to the heart of Rome. Behind the 17th-century exterior, you'll find 34 guest rooms outfitted with rosewood canopy beds and handmade Italian fabrics, sourced and designed by the acclaimed Florentine architect Michele Bönan. Located in a former architecture school, the hotel is an ideal jumping-off point for exploring the city, a stone's throw from the Spanish Steps and fashionable shops on Via Condotti.

30 Via Monte d'Oro; 39-06/9826-3499; jkroma.com. **$$$$**

A Master room at J.K. Place Roma.

First Hotel's rooftop bar, with a view of Rome's city center.

Inside one of Gran Meliá Rome's Premium rooms.

2 First Hotel

Hidden in the *centro storico,* the First Hotel caters to contemporary tastes, favoring sharp edges in its modern roof deck; a glossy white-on-white lobby; and a small, brightly lit bar. The 29 rooms and suites are spacious for Rome (the smallest clocks in at about 220 square feet) and are done up in soft shades of taupe, with dark-marble baths and a carefully edited selection of design and culture books perched on lacquered wooden shelves. Nearby gallery owner Massimiliano Mucciaccia was tapped to curate the hotel's cutting-edge art pieces, including a giant ivory bull statue in the lobby covered with rotary telephones.

14 Via del Vantaggio; 39-06/4561-7070; thefirsthotel.com. **$$$$**

3 Gran Meliá

Ancient Rome may have been famous for its pleasure palaces, but the city has never had a retreat that combines the conveniences of an urban hotel with the soothing accoutrements of a resort. That all changed with the arrival of Gran Meliá. Set on two landscaped acres (Emperor Nero's mother once lived in a villa on the grounds), the hotel's 116 guest rooms have antiqued metal doors, white stone counters, and photographs depicting details of Italian paintings. There are also myriad ways to channel the present day: a tranquil spa, serene outdoor pool, and large stone terrace—the perfect spot for a sunset *aperitivo.*

3 Via del Gianicolo; 888/956-3542; gran-melia.com. **$$$$**

Monaci delle Terre Nere

Monaci delle Terre Nere against the Mount Etna National Park. Opposite: The double Deluxe Floreale Room.

When industrialist Guido Coffa purchased a Baroque villa on a 40-acre
fruit farm at the foot of Mount Etna, transforming it into one of the
most sustainable hotels in Sicily wasn't part of his plan. Yet, six years later,
he's accomplished just that. The walls are cut from local volcanic rock,
the beamed ceilings are made from Etna chestnut wood, and 50 percent
of the hotel's energy is from renewable sources. But that doesn't mean
style has been sacrificed: the 14 sleek rooms mix 18th-century antiques
with larger-than-life paintings by British-Brazilian artist Olivier Mourao
and glossy red lampshades. What we loved best? The thoughtful
touches include mini-bars stocked with regional wines and designer
Philippe Starck's postmodern take on the classic Louis XVI armchair.

Zafferana Etnea; 39-095/708-3638; monacidelleterrenere.it. **$$**

ISTANBUL

Shangri-La Bosphorus

Shangri-La is the newest luxury brand to plant its flag on a ritzy east-bank stretch of the Bosporus, joining the Four Seasons and Kempinski. In the summer months, music from a string quartet greets you at this 1930's former tobacco warehouse; inside you'll find more than 1,000 pieces of original Ottoman art and a three-level atrium capped with a massive Bohemian chandelier. Expect views of the strait from more than half of its 186 guest rooms. In classic Shangri-La fashion, East-meets-West accents appear throughout the property, including at the first European outpost of Chi, the Spa, where Turkish hammams are lined with local tiles and Chinese healing therapies are administered in eight private suites. Alongside the grandiose displays of opulence, two centuries-old sycamore trees that thrive in the courtyard serve as subtle reminders of the building's humble beginnings.

1 Sinanpasa Mah, Hayrettin Iskelesi Sk., Beşiktaş; 866/565-5050; shangri-la.com. **$$$$**

The Shangri-La,
on the banks
of the Bosporus.

One of the guest rooms at the Four Seasons Lion Palace.

ST. PETERSBURG, RUSSIA

Four Seasons Lion Palace

The latest in a string of heritage restorations from Four Seasons, the Lion Palace is the brand's most ambitious project yet. After almost a decade in the works, the 200-year-old structure channels the original building, with soaring ceilings, ivory-painted millwork, all-marble bathrooms, and gilded walnut doors. Also fit for a king: the vodka-and-caviar tasting at Xander Bar, with more than 40 iterations of Russia's favorite spirit. Near St. Isaac's Cathedral and the Hermitage, the building's bright yellow exterior is a revered St. Petersburg landmark. Pushkin certainly thought so: Russia's most famous poet mentioned the palace, and the two lion statues that guard it, in his iconic poem "The Bronze Horseman."

1 Voznesensky Prospekt; 866/630-5890; fourseasons.com. **$$$**

A selection of caviar at Xander Bar. Above: The hotel's imperial exterior.

europe

Sand dunes surrounding
Erg Chigaga Luxury Desert
Camp, in Morocco.

Africa + The Middle East

A cabana at La Sultana Qualidia.

Looking out at the lagoon from the infinity pool. Right: A suite at the hotel.

OUALIDIA, MOROCCO

La Sultana

On the shores of a flamingo-filled lagoon, the small, undeveloped fishing village of Oualidia is the antidote to frenetic Casablanca, 112 miles up the coast. Check in to the waterfront La Sultana Oualidia, with its limestone exterior, high-arched windows, and palm-tree-studded grounds that pay homage to the region's Moorish past. At the hotel's terrace restaurant, guests gather to eat oysters and sip Moroccan wines. In the evenings, a jetty is reserved for private dining, and beachside Berber pavilions host a lively cocktail hour. Whether you're taking in the sunset from your private Jacuzzi or simply stargazing from your terrace, unwinding here is a soul-soothing endeavor.

3 Parc à Huîtres; 212-524/388-008; lasultanahotels.com. **$$$$**

Erg Chigaga Luxury Desert Camp

Amid the saffron-gold dunes of the Sahara lies Erg Chigaga, an authentic desert oasis that provides isolation at its finest. The brainchild of a transplanted English hotel executive, Nick Garsten, and a Moroccan Berber guide, Mohammed Boulfrifri, the eight traditional *caidal* tents have bold red-and-cream-striped walls and thick pile rugs lining the ground. Bathrooms are equipped with hand-worked metal vanities and hot- and cold-water buckets on teak platforms for hammam-style bathing. The camp offers various activities, from sand-boarding and ATV excursions to guided hikes and camel treks. Come evening, rounds of strong mint tea and whiskey are passed around a fire against a backdrop of flickering stars. But the wow factor is the cinematic emptiness.

212-654/395-520; desertcampmorocco.com; all-inclusive. **$$$$**

A king bed inside
a Berber tent at
Erg Chigaga Luxury
Desert Camp.

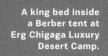

Marrakesh

You'd have to have been living on another planet for the past half-decade not to have clocked the meteoric rise of the Red City. While five-star resorts have sprung up in and around Marrakesh, inside the medina's chiaroscuro labyrinth of alleys and lanes, chic *riad*s have elevated standards for Moroccan design and service. With these urbane and luxurious properties, the city now feels like a place where nothing is beyond reach.

1 Four Seasons Resort Marrakech

Looking for a quiet retreat away from the hubbub of the medina? This resort in Hivernage, a neighborhood just minutes from downtown, has Moorish gardens and flawless service. A strong sense of place emerges throughout the property, from the 141 rooms outfitted with locally crafted wood furnishings to the spicy lamb *tagine* at Solano restaurant. An on-site cultural center offers crash courses in Arabic calligraphy. The trump card? Healing rituals at Le Spa.

1 Blvd. de la Menara; 800/819-5053; fourseasons.com. **$$$$**

Palms flank the grounds at Four Seasons Resort Marrakech.

Taj Palace Marrakech's Jade Room.

Outside a suite at Riad Abracadabra.

▣ Riad Abracadabra

Don't be deterred by the quirky name; Barcelona-born cousins Inés and Bruno's refurbished *riad* in the medina, just steps from Djemaa el-Fna square, was once a mansion for a family of aristocrats. Beyond the entrance, you'll find an inviting indoor-outdoor lounge, with plush cream-colored couches around a gurgling fountain. The bi-level, colonial-style rooms have whitewashed walls and bookshelves stacked with novels and vintage design magazines. For knockout views of the Atlas Mountains, head to the rooftop deck, dotted with daybeds and tented sitting areas—perfect for pre-dinner cocktails.

125 Derb Jamaa; 212-524/384-039; riadabracadabra.com. **$$**

▣ Taj Palace Marrakech

The Taj brand's Moroccan *pièce de résistance* was seven years in the making, and its sheer grandeur—aptly reflected by the Murano glass chandelier dangling from the two-story atrium—raises the bar for a city already teeming with impressive hotels. A mix of Asian, Moroccan, and Ottoman influences is on display in the 161 rooms; there are Swarovski-studded curtains, mirrored and frescoed ceilings, hothouse-palette Indian textiles, and gold leaf, all juxtaposed with hundreds of antique Berber rugs. The on-site spa, which emphasizes couples treatments, spans 40,000 square feet.

Annakhil, Palmeraie; 800/819-5053; tajhotels.com. **$$$$**

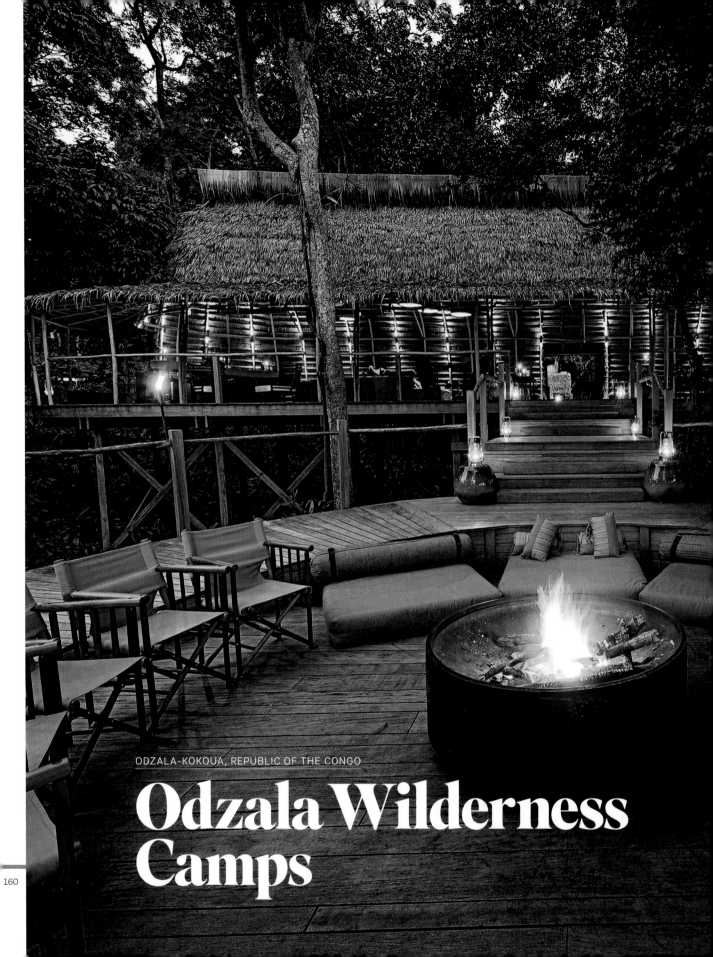

ODZALA-KOKOUA, REPUBLIC OF THE CONGO

Odzala Wilderness Camps

One of Lango Camp's six suites. Opposite: A fire pit at Ngaga Camp.

Northern Congo's Odzala-Kokoua—part of the second largest rain forest in the world—has forest elephants, and a handful of Pygmy tribes, but few travelers. Now Wilderness Safaris is pulling back the curtain on the region's first high-end safari camp. It has two environmentally minded lodges—Lango Camp, on the edge of the savanna, and Ngaga Camp, set deep in the rain forest; each consists of six nature-inspired suites, dressed in bamboo and decorated with Congolese crafts and artifacts. Leather and canvas furniture and wraparound terraces add creature comforts. The real draw, however, is Odzala's unrivaled access to its wild neighbors, particularly the 35 resident gorillas who live just outside your door.

Odzala-Kokoua National Park; 27-11/807-1800; wilderness-safaris.com; six-night minimum. $$$$$

Dusk at
Chinzombo,
near the
Luangwa River.

SOUTH LUANGWA, ZAMBIA

Chinzombo

Designed with clean, straight lines and crisp canvas trappings, riverside
Chinzombo stands out from other Zambian lodges for its stylish austerity.
This section of the roiling Luangwa River is known for Thornicroft's
giraffes, along with copious elephants and hippos, which veteran guide
Abraham Banda regards with impressive equanimity. Burnished
copper accents jazz up the six freestanding suites (each with a private
plunge pool and sweeping deck), accessible to guests via antique wooden
doors imported from China. Sawhorse tables, recycled timber floors,
and white campaign chairs add an upscale-colonial feel to the main
lodge, while the curios on display—ranging from a huge antique crocodile
skull to photos of safari legend Norman Carr with his pet lions, circa 1970—
are rich with history.

Chinzombo; 260-216/246-015. **$$$$$**

A tent at Selinda
Explorers Camp.

The central dining pavilion. Left: Canoes on the Selinda Spillway.

Selinda Explorers Camp

There's nothing inauthentic about this exceedingly private, eco-friendly camp on the banks of the Selinda Spillway, an ancient channel that doubles as headquarters for the region's wildlife (it's frequented by throngs of elephants, buffalo, antelope, wildebeests, and zebras). The four custom-designed tents, furnished with hardwoods and regional art, rely entirely on a UV filtration system for water. Choose from an array of adventures: canoe rides, swims among high reeds in the Spillway, or 4 x 4 excursions on which you might glimpse a wild dog, one of Africa's most endangered predators. Come nightfall, recount your sightings over a glass of Amarula by the bonfire.

Selinda Reserve; 425/392-0163; greatplains conservation.com; all-inclusive. **$$$$$**

africa + the middle east

Singita Mara River Tented Camp

The standard-bearer for luxury safaris, Singita is once again redefining in-the-bush experiences with the debut of its first camp in the unspoiled northwestern corner of the Serengeti. Six sunrise-facing tents, courtesy of renowned Cape Town–based design team Cécile & Boyd's, showcase native crafts, such as decorative baskets reminiscent of grain-sorting containers and throw blankets with Masai-inspired patterns. Days begin with predawn game drives and end with sundowners on the plains. Guests can linger all day with a cup of English Breakfast on their patios, where a pair of high-powered binoculars aids in viewing animals along the Mara River. Since the property runs entirely on solar energy, rest assured that the only footprints left behind will be those of elephants, hippos, and—if you go in late summer—thousands of migrating wildebeests.

Lamai Triangle; 27-21/683-3424; singita.com; meals included. **$$$$$**

The plunge pool in Singita Mara River's main camp.

LAIKIPIA, KENYA

Segera Retreat

In central Kenya's Laikipia Plateau—along with an untrammeled alternative to the Masai Mara—the lush Segera was born out of a collaboration between former Puma CEO and environmentalist Jochen Zeitz and the Wilderness Collection of African lodges. The property takes its community engagement seriously, offering guests the opportunity to help with reforestation efforts or to monitor the area's population of endangered patas monkeys and Grevy's zebras. Along with these hands-on excursions, there are expert-led wildlife tours around the 50,000 acres of privately owned savanna. The eight villas, with their thatched roofs, ebony interiors, and contemporary art, do not compromise on luxury.

Nanyuki; 254-20/619-0800; segera.com; all-inclusive. **$$$$**

The staff sets up
a picnic on the
grounds. Opposite:
A villa garden
swing bed.

Animals surround Mahali Mzuri's terra-cotta-colored suites.

MASAI MARA, KENYA

Mahali Mzuri

As the latest addition to the Virgin Limited Edition collection, this futuristic riff on the traditional East African safari—the 12 terra-cotta-hued suites, encircled by steel girders, are reminiscent of spaceships—blends a boutique-hotel sensibility with natural beauty. Some classic tropes, including canopied beds, claw-foot tubs, and handmade Kenyan textiles are on display, but playful touches such as sea-urchin-shaped lights, a spear that doubles as a Do Not Disturb sign, and rubber ducks in Masai garb deliver plenty of Branson whimsy. Guests devour grilled meats and fresh salads (courtesy of the on-site garden) on a glamorous glass table studded with votive candles. And for wildlife-spotting, there's no better perch than the cliff-edge infinity pool.

Olare Motorgi Conservancy; 877/577-8777; mahalimzuri.virgin.com; all-inclusive. **$$$$$**

The pool at
the St. Regis
Mauritius
Resort.

An ocean-view room. Right: The hotel's colonial staircase.

St. Regis Mauritius Resort

Out in the Indian Ocean, 1,250 miles east of Africa, the tiny isle of Mauritius—long a getaway for wealthy Indians and Europeans—is known for its over-the-top resorts. And the St. Regis doesn't disappoint. The 172 rooms, set in colonial-style villas, are decorated in milky hues and warm woods and overlook the Morne peninsula or the glittering sea. The most spectacular are the Grand suites, where spacious balconies include handcrafted wooden daybeds. Turn to the hotel's expert staff for advice on what to do around the island, from a skydiving adventure to a tour of a nearby rum factory and Chinese cooking classes at the property's Floating Market restaurant.

Le Morne; 877/788-3447; stregis.com. **$$$$$**

UNITED ARAB EMIRATES

Oberoi Dubai

The location—a business district still under development—leaves something to be desired, but upon checking in to the new Oberoi Dubai all is forgiven. Deep soaking tubs, butler-delivered chocolate truffles, complimentary poolside yoga classes, a contemporary Indian restaurant, and other amenities make the property a standout, even by gilded Dubai's excessive standards. And in a city obsessed with superlatives, it's hard to believe there's room for another first, but the Oberoi throws its hat into the ring with Dubai's only 24-hour spa.

Oberoi Center, Business Bay; 800/562-3764; oberoihotels.com. $$$

The infinity pool at
the Oberoi Dubai.

Al Sahel Villa Resort

The Middle East may not be the first place that comes to mind when you think *safari*, but Anantara's Al Sahel hopes to change that. Located within the 10,380-acre Arabian Wildlife Park, the rustic-luxe lodge offers its guests an up-close look at the animals (some 10,000) that inhabit the area, including endangered Arabian oryx, sand gazelles, cheetahs, and hyenas. Each of the 30 thatched-roof cottages has a bamboo four-poster bed and carved wooden bathtub and washbasins, but for the ultimate haute-safari experience, book one of the two-bedroom villas, so you can watch from your own plunge pool as the wildlife roam over salt-domed hilltops. Immerse yourself further in the setting with a nature walk or an archaeological tour led by the hotel's expert guides.

Sir Bani Yas Island; 971/2801-5400; al-sahel.anantara.com. **$$$$**

One of Al Sahel's pool villas. Opposite: A cottage with panoramic savanna views.

DOHA, QATAR

St. Regis

There's no question—Doha is poised to emerge on the global stage, thanks to its I. M. Pei–designed Museum of Islamic Art and 2024 Olympics plans. Upping the city's luxury ante is the new 336-room St. Regis. The property evokes the brand's century-old Manhattan roots with more than its Fifth Avenue–worthy style: it's also home to the first international outpost of Jazz at Lincoln Center, overseen by artistic director Wynton Marsalis. Add to this two Gordon Ramsay restaurants, a Remède spa, and butler service fit for a sheikh, and the place is hard to resist.

West Bay; 877/787-3447; stregis.com. **$$$**

The Olympic-size pool at the St. Regis Doha.

One of the Alma
Hotel's Executive
suites.

TEL AVIV

Alma Hotel & Lounge

To see what really makes Tel Aviv tick, head to the White City UNESCO World Heritage site, where design and architecture take center stage. Smack in the middle of it all, the Alma Hotel & Lounge has become the discerning traveler's hotel of choice. Siblings Adi and Irit Strauss have created a patchwork of bohemian luxury in 15 airy rooms inspired by the 1920's, each with bijou stained-glass windows and handwoven carpets. Yonatan Roshfeld, the chef behind nearby tapas hot spot Ahad Haám, lures Israeli socialites and Russian businessmen to the hotel's namesake restaurant with Moroccan small plates (beet-topped raw beef *kibbeh* in sheep's milk; lamb encrusted with red pepper, roasted garlic, thyme, and sage). The artful menu perfectly complements the décor, which is lifted straight out of Paris's Marais district: a smattering of jewel-toned chairs, checkered floors, and edgy contemporary artwork.

23 Yavne St.; 972-3/630-8777; almahotel.co.il. **$$$**

Alma Lounge.
Above: The hotel's renovated 1920's exterior.

The living room
at Uma by Como,
Paro, in Bhutan

Asia

The Tokyo Station
Hotel's contemporary
lobby. Opposite:
The hotel's setting
in Marunouchi.

Tokyo Station Hotel

Nary a bullet-train rumble can be heard from the 150 serene rooms of the Tokyo Station Hotel—a surprise, given that the property sits above Japan's busiest railway hub. Located in the renovated Tokyo Station Marunouchi Building, one of the few remaining examples of pre–World War II architecture in the city, the hotel reopened after an exhaustive six-year overhaul that restored century-old details, including the ornate yellow domes in the lobby. The Tokyo Station Hotel delivers all the modern amenities you could hope for (Toto toilets; goose-down-topped beds; mini-bars stocked with top-shelf Hibiki whiskey), but the clincher is that you're a short stroll from the Imperial Palace and just steps from rail lines that connect to all corners of the country.

1-9-1 Marunouchi; 81-3/5220-1111; thetokyostationhotel.jp. $$

The lounge in
Chalet Ivy's
reception area.

A guest room with views of Mount Yotei. Above: En route to the Hirafu slopes.

Chalet Ivy

The island of Hokkaido is a mecca for skiers: famous for its dry, fluffy powder, it receives 50 feet of snowfall a year. Bunk down at the new Chalet Ivy, with its 33 guest rooms, some of which overlook Mount Yotei, and marble *onsen* bath fed by a hot spring that simmers 1,640 feet underground. Though winter is prime time here, every season has something to offer. When the weather warms, there's biking, horseback riding, hiking, and rafting, plus visits to the Chalet Ivy Private Farm, where guests can pick their own produce for dinner at the hotel's farm-to-table restaurant, Snow Castle.

188-19 Yamada, Kutchan; 81-136/221-123; chaletivy.com. **$$$**

asia

The lobby at
East. Opposite:
A sunset view
of the hotel.

BEIJING

East

If Beijing is China's creative hub, then this hotel perfectly embodies Beijing. Step inside the 25-story glass tower in the city's Chaoyang business district and you'll find some of the young staff in hoodies and a media center equipped with a video wall showcasing contemporary local art that operates more like a corner café. That's where tech entrepreneurs and young movers and shakers mingle over lattes. The 369 sleek guest rooms have muted hues and iPod Touches; downstairs, there's a standout Japanese restaurant and a lounge with live music and 180 premium whiskeys.

22 Jiuxianqiao Rd.; 86-10/8426-0888; east-beijing.com. $

asia

189

SHANGHAI

Banyan Tree
Shanghai
on the Bund

The hotel's indoor lap pool.

Though a visit to this megalopolis of 23 million feels overwhelming, Banyan Tree's first Shanghai property, on the northern part of the iconic Bund waterfront, can provide the ultimate escape. Take the 130 enormous guest rooms—among the city's largest—all with chaise longues offering unobstructed views of the Huangpu River. Then there's the service, both thoughtful and swift, from the laundry pickup via a valet box by your door to the attentive concierge, who can book you one of the hotel's glitzy gold cabs to shuttle around town. The showstopper, however, is the three-floor, marble-clad spa, spread across 14,000 square feet, with a treatment menu so comprehensive that it would take months to fully experience.

19 Hai Ping Rd · 800/591-0439; banyantree.com. $$$

Anantara Xishuangbanna Resort & Spa

Guests at Anantara Xishuangbanna may feel they are in tropical Thailand, not southwestern China—this 80-suite, 23-villa resort is only 40 miles from the infamous Golden Triangle. Set in a delicate oasis of wild orchids on the Luosuo River, the verdant property is a coveted spot for Shanghai and Beijing residents seeking five-star treatment. Interiors are lined with gold inlay work and lotus motifs inspired by the local Dai tribe—one of the 12 minority communities that make up this region. And Sinophiles won't be disappointed: traditional wooden courtyards surround villas with private swimming pools, while the Manfeilong Pagoda (a historic stupa complex built in 1024), which resembles an elegant stack of bamboo shoots, is just 30 minutes away.

Menglun Town; 86-691/893-6666; anantara.com. **$$$**

Anantara Xishuangbanna's main pool. Opposite: Inside a villa at the resort.

A waiting
lounge outside
the hotel's
barber shop.

Mandarin Oriental

A $150 million stem-to-stern renovation has renewed the luster of this legendary property—a decades-long favorite of such visiting dignitaries as Margaret Thatcher and Henry Kissinger. Many of the 501 rooms have been enlarged, and high-tech amenities—touch-screen lighting and temperature control, for example—have been added. The décor has been updated, too, with plush velvety fabrics, wood wall panels, and colorfully glazed Asian ceramics. Though there's a spa spanning three floors with Chinese herbal steam rooms, bathing beauties may be perfectly content to relax in their own airy marble bathrooms, kitted out with Hermès toiletries. The real choice comes in the form of 10 separate restaurants and bars. Our favorites: Man Wah, with its classic Cantonese cuisine, and the French-influenced Pierre.

5 Connaught Rd.; 800/526-6566; mandarinoriental.com. **$$$$**

asia

195

Mira Moon Hotel

Acclaimed Dutch designer Marcel Wanders, dubbed the Lady Gaga of interiors, has applied his signature playful aesthetic to the new Mira Moon, in Hong Kong's fashionable Wan Chai neighborhood. The look is loosely inspired by the mythical Moon Goddess and Jade Rabbit, characters from a well-known Chinese Moon Festival story. Bold hues and intricate patterns—colorful mosaics, splashy rugs, and ornate chandeliers—are woven through the dramatic lobby, restaurant, spa, and 91 rooms. Every detail has been considered here, from the fragrance that permeates the public spaces (violet) to the staff's bespoke chinoiserie outfits and hairdos (created by local designer Grace Choi and a dedicated on-staff stylist, respectively). Charmed by what you see? You can purchase select furnishings and fashions featured in the hotel and have them shipped home.

388 Jaffe Rd.; 852/2643-8888; miramoonhotel.com. **$$**

A street view of Mira Moon at dusk. Opposite: One of the hotel's Full Moon rooms.

asia

197

Strolling on a
deck with views
of Bacuit Bay.

Local seafood at the hotel's restaurant, Amianan. Below: A guest villa.

PALAWAN, PHILIPPINES

El Nido Resorts

In the Palawan archipelago, the tiny private island of Pangulasian is home to the latest and most luxurious entry in the expanding El Nido Resorts collection. Forty-two airy thatched-roof villas—some close to the sound of lapping waves—are steps from a ribbon of soft white sand. Behind you is a canopy of green; before you is limpid blue Bacuit Bay, part of a UNESCO-protected biosphere reserve. Swim 10 yards out and you'll be floating with turtles and parrot fish above a pristine coral reef. Or kayak to one of the several nearby islands and claim your own sun-drenched shore. Back at the resort, a traditional *hilot* massage awaits, along with fresh coconuts retrieved by staffers who climb 30-foot-tall trees to pick them.

Pangulasian Island; 63-2/813-0000; elnidoresorts.com. $$$$

INDONESIA

Regent Bali

You'll find a warm, residential vibe at the Regent Bali, hidden on 10 acres of tropical beachfront in mellow Sanur. Eschewing the timber-and-terrazzo design found in many Bali resorts, the hotel's interiors incorporate native materials such as Indonesian marble, natural shells, and Bangkirai wood. The spa, too, draws inspiration from what's found on-island in treatments such as a coffee polish, a massage with cajeput oil, and baths scented with frangipani, champac, and ylang-ylang. Your biggest decision here? Which indulgence to opt for: a yoga session by the ocean, a dip in the infinity pool, or a fresh fruit cocktail in the on-site library bar.

8 Jalan Kusama Sari, Sanur Beach; 866/630-5890; regenthotels.com. **$$$**

Regent Bali's
beachfront
swimming pool.

Multistory vertical gardens at Park Royal.

A birdcage-style cabana by Park Royal's infinity pool. Right: The hotel's lobby.

Park Royal on Pickering

Thanks to a curvy façade that's draped with a riot of greenery, the Park Royal cuts a distinctive profile at the gateway to Singapore's Central Business District. Conceived by local architecture firm Woha, the building showcases sustainable design, with solar panels on the roof and four stories of undulating planters topped with sleek blue-and-green glass towers. Enter the property and you'll forget that you're in the center of one of the world's densest cities: it has reflecting ponds, stepping stones, waterfalls, an elevated walking path, and a cabana-lined infinity pool. Just beyond the hotel lies the oldest Hindu temple in Singapore and the chic bars and cafés of the Ann Siang Hill neighborhood.

3 Upper Pickering St.; 800/255-7795; parkroyalhotels.com. $$

asia

Macalister Mansion

A guest room at
Macalister Mansion.
Opposite: Café
tables on the lawn.

Take a 100-year-old manor house, add mid-20th-century furnishings, life-size animal sculptures, and large bathtubs lined with silver mosaic tiles, and you've got Malaysia's most stylish new hotel. Located on the island of Penang—home of the UNESCO-designated 18th-century George Town—the eight-room Macalister Mansion references the destination's colonial past, but with a bold nod to the future. To wit: the entrance's eight-foot-high resin bust of the first British governor of Penang. In the evening, a 20-minute taxi ride brings you to the center of George Town to explore one of Southeast Asia's most exciting street-food scenes, or linger at the hotel's stately Cellar bar, which has Penang's largest wine collection (over 300 labels).

228 Jalan Macalister; 60-4/228-3888; macalistermansion.com. **$$**

A view of Vana Belle from the Gulf of Thailand.

KOH SAMUI, THAILAND

Vana Belle

In ancient Sanskrit, *vana* means "magical forest"—a fitting moniker for this idyllic hotel in Koh Samui, set on a lushly wooded cove. Built around existing calabash trees and rock formations, the resort exudes an authentic sense of place, from the indigenous ritual that greets you upon arrival to the mouthwatering southern Thai cuisine at the hilltop Kiree restaurant; try the *yam pak good* (wild tropical ferns topped with tiger prawns and grated coconut). The 80 suites and villas have granite-lined bathrooms and private pools and terraces, plus original artwork that depicts fanciful creatures from local lore. And though the hotel feels far-flung, you're actually just a short drive from the airport and the island's most jaw-dropping waterfalls and natural pools.

9/99 Moo 3, Chaweng Noi Beach, Surat Thani; 800/325-3589; vanabellekohsamui.com. **$$$$**

The hotel's Ocean View Pool Suite. Above: A traditional *kunchorn waree* sculpture.

Uma by Como, Paro

With its pristine landscapes and well-preserved Buddhist temples, eastern Bhutan has had little in the way of stylish retreats. Enter this offering by Como hotels, in the untouched Paro Valley. The sleek sister property to Uma by Como, Punakha, in western Bhutan, Paro is a welcome respite between long treks through the Himalayas. Nine guest rooms designed by Malaysian-born Cheong Yew Kuan (also behind Bali's Como Shambhala Estate) are decked out in native blue pine, while floor-to-ceiling windows overlook rolling green hills. A breakfast of ginger-and-lime muffins with house-made watermelon jam fortifies guests for trips to Punakha Dzong Monastery, one of the country's most important sites—a 25-minute hike away along the lush valley's rim.

Paro; 975-8/271-597; comohotels.com. **$$$$$**

A massage room at the hotel spa. Opposite: Rice terraces at the retreat.

Exploring Bardia
National Park
by elephant.

Pomegranate-infused sorbet at the lodge's restaurant. Right: Relaxing on a guest room terrace.

NEPAL

Tiger Tops Karnali Lodge

A decade-long civil war discouraged many adventurers from visiting the vast Himalayan peaks that dominate Nepal's horizon, but a 2006 peace treaty put this hiker's nirvana back on the bucket list. A three-hour trip from Kathmandu, the recently renovated Tiger Tops Karnali Lodge, bordering Bardia National Park, seems worlds away from the frenetic capital. Immerse yourself in the abundant wildlife: guided treks wend through the Babai Valley, past herds of elephants, one-horned rhinos, and swamp deer. You'll return from your expedition to one of nine intimate, earth-toned suites, powered almost entirely by solar energy. Come evening, enjoy a Ghorka beer at the bar— open until the last guest retires—where you just might overhear the unmistakable chuffing of the elusive Bengal tiger.

Bardia National Park; 977-1/441-1225; tigertops.com; all-inclusive. **$$$**

Dusit Devarana

Lifestyle executives at Dusit Devarana New Delhi. Opposite: The hotel's 335-foot pool.

Off a frenzied stretch of the National Highway, the Dusit Devarana is an unlikely urban oasis, thanks to its 7½ acres of manicured lawns, massive stone columns inspired by those at the Elephanta Caves near Mumbai, and a 335-foot swimming pool (the longest in the city). Each of the 50 rooms comes with a "lifestyle executive," or private butler, who can swiftly arrange for personalized shopping tours of Dilli Haat, a handicrafts market in South Delhi, or chauffeur-driven trips to the storied Baha'i Lotus Temple. Crowds regularly flock to the hotel's outdoor café Kiyan for its contemporary Thai dishes, like the steamed Chilean sea bass in cilantro broth and tenderloin salad, spiked with bird's-eye chiles.

8 National Hwy., Makarpura, Samalka; 91-11/3355-2211; dusit.com. $$

Mumbai

Vast, teeming, and electrifying, Mumbai (Bombay, to locals) is the quintessential Indian megalopolis. Aggressively modern yet medieval, glamorous but humble—contradictions are inherent to its identity. For proof, look to the palace-like hotels scattered across the city. Here, three of our favorites.

1 Taj Mahal Palace

A 1903 grande dame overlooking the 85-foot-high Gateway of India, the iconic Taj Mahal Palace has a long and storied history. In 2010, two years after bombings damaged much of the structure, the reopening was cause for a countrywide celebration. The lobby of the plush Edwardian palace— vaulted ceilings; silk carpets; onyx columns; etched glasswork— has a new contemporary look, but the heritage wing's 285 rooms and suites—each with its own butler—remain reassuringly classic.

Apollo Bunder; 866/969-1825; tajhotels.com. **$$$**

The Taj Mahal Palace's pool area.

A Sofitel Mumbai guest room.

Breakfast at Palladium Hotel's Seven restaurant.

2 Sofitel Mumbai BKC

Set in the city's Bandra Kurla Complex, this 14-story glass building is the work of Singapore-based designer Isabelle Miaja, who puts a playful spin on Indian- and French-inspired motifs. There's a huge bronze elephant statue on the fourth floor and eight-foot-tall totem poles embellished with tigers and Eiffel Towers in the lobby. The rooms are more subtle, with neutral tones and dark wood floors. If the hyper-attentive service doesn't win you over, the culinary offerings surely will: red curry at Pondichery Café, Rajasthani fare at Tuskers, handmade sweets at the bakery Artisan, or a tandoori feast at Jyran.

BKC Rd., Bandra Kurla Complex, C-57, Bandra; 800/763-4835; sofitel.com. **$**

3 Palladium Hotel

Mumbai's newest kid on the block is adding even more prestige to the Lower Parel neighborhood, which once housed the city's textile mills. The lobby's Botticino-marble staircase is flanked by gilded mirrors and wall sconces bejeweled with crystal. Upstairs, the 390 well-appointed guest rooms incorporate traditional Indian flourishes such as *tikri* artwork, and have sweeping views of the Arabian Sea. If it's sartorial inspiration you're after, don't miss the ground-floor Palladium Mall, filled with high-end local and international boutiques: Amber & Shirrin, Gucci, and Ashmina, to name a few.

462 High St. Phoenix, Senapati Bapat Marg, Lower Parel; 866/565-5050; shangri-la.com. **$$**

HYDERABAD, INDIA

Park Hyatt

A sitting room in one of the hotel's furnished apartments.

The Indian home base for Facebook and Google, Hyderabad draws a legion of global execs—and the latest high-tech, high-style retreat is destined to become a hot spot for them all. With a central location in upscale Banjara Hills, the hotel offers all the amenities a business traveler could hope for (seamless in-room check-in; round-the-clock concierge service; safes that fit your laptop). Hand-laid walnut floors and stand-alone tubs add grandeur to each of the 209 rooms and 42 luxury apartments, while the 14,500-square-foot spa includes a Swarovski-crystal mirror. If you're stuck inside during one of the city's notorious summer monsoons, head to the lush indoor garden that seems to hover over the soaring lobby.

Rd. No. 2, Banjara Hills; 800/233-1234; park.hyatt.com. $

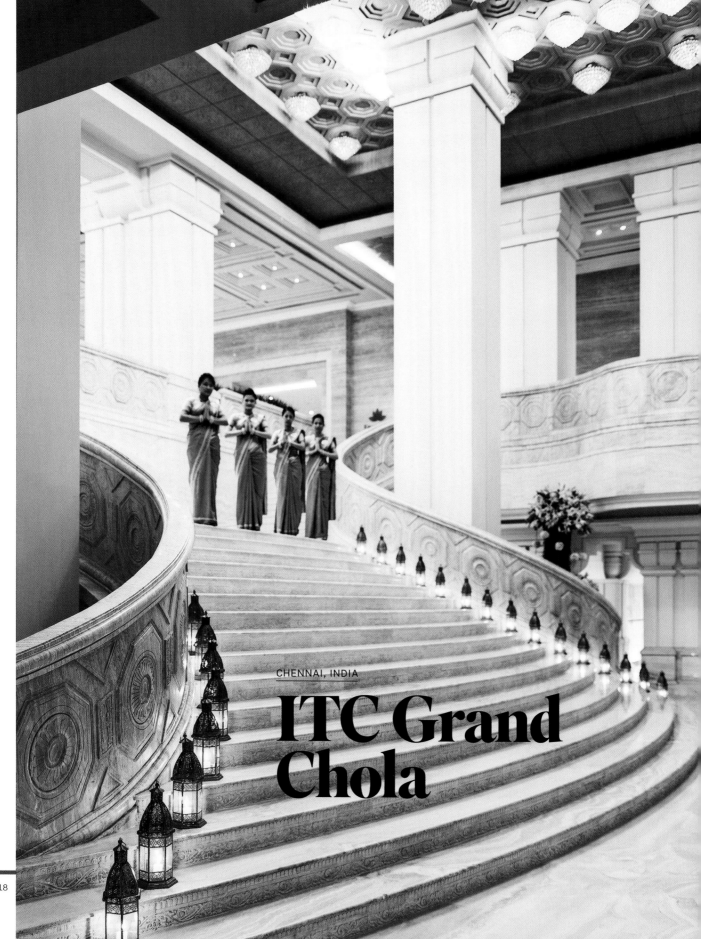

CHENNAI, INDIA

ITC Grand Chola

A grand, honey-colored marble staircase welcomes guests to the ITC Grand Chola, leading them past a series of glazed-glass doors lit by crystal chandeliers. Elegant staffers in saris guide visitors as Indian pipe music fills the air. On the second floor, guests kick back at the Kaya Kalp Spa, where they can enjoy synchronized massages, courtesy of two therapists simultaneously applying a blend of Eastern and Western techniques with the same pressure and speed. Gentlemen receive hot Sicilian shaves while relaxing in imported Italian barber chairs at the Salon de Willis. Other highlights: a cigar and whiskey lounge and a carefully curated art gallery that channels the ancient Chola dynasty's passion for bronze sculptures.

63 Mount Rd.; 91-44/2220-0000; itchotels.in. **$$**

The property's palatial exterior. Opposite: Staffers on the hotel staircase.

COORG, INDIA

Vivanta by Taj

For decades, in-the-know Bangaloreans have flocked to the region of Coorg, in the southwestern state of Karnataka, for its mist-shrouded rain forests, rolling coffee plantations, and off-the-grid vibe. Now, with the opening of Vivanta by Taj Madikeri, this undiscovered area has landed on the global traveler's map. The five-hour drive from Bangalore may be long, but a glimpse of the staggering vistas from the open-air lobby provides instant relief—as do the 57 cottages. All are modeled after traditional Coorgi homes, with vaulted ceilings, doors made from coconut shells, and large picture windows. The ultimate goal here is to unwind, and the resort's 180 acres have a variety of soothing pastimes, from clay-sculpting sessions to a bath in a wood-fired Gudda tub (still found in some local dwellings) in the outdoor pavilion.

First Monnangeri, Galibeedu Post Madikeri; 866/969-1825; vivantabytaj.com. **$$**

The resort's
skylit pool.

Lofty ceilings
in an Island villa
at Cheval Blanc
Randheli.

Lounge chairs by a private pool. Right: Preparing for lunch in an outdoor pergola.

MALDIVES

Cheval Blanc Randheli

Overwater bungalows may be a dime a dozen in the Maldives, but Cheval Blanc Randheli, on the unspoiled Noonu Atoll, is something truly extraordinary. The property is managed by LVMH Hotel Management, so its style credentials are solid. Transport to the hotel is via a private seaplane painted a jaunty yellow and taupe and stocked with welcome gifts for arriving guests, including towels and espadrilles. Created by architect Jean-Michel Gathy, the 45 villas are fashionably spare, with open floor plans; thatched, cathedral-style bamboo ceilings; and private decks with infinity pools. After a day spent reef snorkeling or cruising on the house yacht, relax with a tailored Guerlain spa treatment, such as the After Diving Experience, designed to improve circulation after you return from the waves.

Noonu Atoll; 960/656-1515; chevalblanc.com.
$$$$$

Bivalves at
the Oyster Inn,
in Auckland,
New Zealand.

Australia+ New Zealand

Cicada Lodge

The 500 remaining Jawoyn Aborigines in the Northern Territory make up one of the world's oldest surviving cultures, and now, with the opening of Cicada Lodge, they're also Australia's most anticipated new hoteliers. Their goal is twofold: put Nitmiluk Gorge—with its carved canyons of ancient sandstone towering over the Katherine River—on the traveler's map, and use the lodge as a means of preserving Jawoyn heritage. Here, 18 airy rooms in muted shades of green and brown incorporate Aboriginal art. If you are drawn to high-octane pursuits (four-wheel-drive touring, say), you've found your place. But there are plenty of less demanding activities, including swimming below pristine waterfalls and helicoptering to historic rock-art sites that date back 20,000 years— all under the direction of these local guides.

61-8/8974-3100; cicadalodge.com.au. $$$$

The gorge at Nitmiluk National Park. Opposite: Cicada Lodge's outdoor pool.

Bedarra Island Resort

Before reopening in July 2013, Bedarra's owners not only restored natural beauty to this 110-acre retreat in Great Barrier Reef Marine Park, but also embraced a more sustainable, eco-friendly ethos. The old diesel generator and desalination plant were ditched; the number of villas was sliced from 16 to seven; and any vestiges of resort-style starchiness were banished, creating a quintessentially Aussie tropical getaway. Fortunately, the well-stocked, help-yourself bar and exclusivity remain. Take a boat ride to a shell-strewn beach with a picnic of organic goodies and a bottle of champagne, or just sit on your villa's private deck and spot turtles swimming in the Coral Sea.

61-7/4068-8233; bedarra.com.au; all-inclusive. **$$$$**

A sunlit porch outside the Point Villa at Bedarra Island Resort.

australia+new zealand

Gwinganna Lifestyle Retreat

Americans are just starting to discover Australia's Gold Coast, a beachside city in Queensland that's been a favorite of Oz's A-list for years. Make your base the new Gwinganna Lifestyle Retreat (co-owned by actor Hugh Jackman), overlooking the area's rolling valleys. With 55 cottages, suites, and villas spread out over 500 acres, this is more than just a wellness resort. Sure, it offers healthful meals, yoga, hiking, and tennis—but where else can you try cricket and stick-fighting, take scenic walks into the bush, and watch a parade of wallabies as the sun sets? The 16,000-square-foot spa (the largest in the Southern Hemisphere) is known for its outside-the-box treatments: try the "rockupuncture," a fusion of hot-stone therapy and acupuncture, or the Australian Spirit of Sound treatment, in which a massage therapist plays a drum and shakes a rain stick, invigorating guests' minds and bodies.

Tallebudgera Valley; 61-7/5589-5000; gwinganna.com; all-inclusive; two-night minimum. $$$$

One of Gwinganna's Signature villas. Opposite: A timber-clad guest room.

BAROSSA VALLEY, AUSTRALIA

Kingsford Homestead

A Georgian-style sandstone house in South Australia's wine country, this homestead has a storied history; once the residence of a wealthy 19th-century British settler, it passed through various hands and served as the set of the popular Australian television show *McLeod's Daughters* in the early 2000's. Today the place has taken on a new role: an all-inclusive luxury inn with seven suites (each named after a former owner), an atmospheric old cellar (the site of nightly local wine tastings), and a tranquil swimming pool. In addition to enjoying hearty breakfasts and multicourse dinners, guests can go hot-air ballooning, paragliding, or hiking, then unwind with a signature "bush bath"—an outdoor soak in a cast-iron claw-foot tub at the edge of the North Para River.

Kingsford; 61-8/8524-8120; kingsfordhomestead.com.au; all-inclusive; two-night minimum. **$$$$**

A view of Kingsford Homestead, on the Barossa Valley's western edge.

Auckland, New Zealand

If you're looking for the appeal of a small town and the sensibility of a modern metropolis, head to Auckland. The city's unique and endearing Kiwi spirit is on display in the countless seaside inns and sleek boutique hotels that stretch from the Central Business District to Waiheke Island. Here, three of our favorites.

1 Hotel DeBrett

In the Central Business District, you'll find the funky DeBrett, one of Auckland's first inns. Owners Michelle Deery and John Courtney rescued the mid-19th-century building from disrepair seven years ago and transformed it into the city's hottest hotel and restaurant. The 25 rooms are a riot of graphic carpets and Midcentury furniture upholstered in orange and turquoise. At night, the revived Housebar is the go-to spot for classic cocktails; order the DeBrett Mule or a Barbados Sour and take in the scene.

2 High St.;
64-9/925-9000;
hoteldebrett.com. **$$**

Diners at DeBrett's Kitchen, in the Hotel DeBrett.

FISH & CHIPPERY

The Oyster Inn's chef, Christian Hossack.

Oyster Inn

Just 35 minutes from Auckland by ferry, Waiheke Island is the Montauk of New Zealand, and combines the breezy ambience of your prototypical seaside town (beach shacks made of cast-off wood; laid-back residents) with a sophisticated edge. The area's latest place to bed down? The Oyster Inn, a three-room retreat that is reminiscent of the rustic houses, or baches, that dot the island. Set in a Victorian-style newspaper office, the rooms are small but sweet, all whitewashed walls and colorful kilims. Don't miss lunch at the patio café, which serves heaping platters of bivalves plucked straight from the sea.

124 Ocean View Rd., Waiheke Island; 64-9/372-2222; theoysterinn.co.nz. **$$**

The Boatshed

It's hard to picture a more appealing island inn than the Boatshed, a complex of five suites and two timber bungalows a stone's throw from a pristine stretch of sand on Waiheke Island. If you come, pack light: all the requisite beach gear is provided in-room, including a shade umbrella, sun hats, tote, and sunscreen. The three Boatshed suites open onto a garden, but for maximum privacy and great views, book the Lighthouse, with its own veranda high above the gulf and a telescope to watch sailboats along the coastline. The best way to navigate the island? Aboard the Mini Moke—a beach buggy available only to guests.

Tawa and Huia Streets, Waiheke Island; 64-9/372-3242; boatshed.co.nz. **$$$$**

World's Best Awards

The Top 100 Hotels

1 **Mombo Camp and Little Mombo Camp**
Moremi Game Reserve, Botswana 96.60

2 **Castello di Casole—A Timbers Resort**
Casole d'Elsa, Italy 96.18

3 **Singita Kruger National Park**
South Africa 96.14

4 **Nayara Hotel, Spa & Gardens**
La Fortuna, Costa Rica 96.14

5 **Four Seasons Resort**
Bora-Bora, French Polynesia 96.00

5 **Lodge at Kauri Cliffs**
Matauri Bay, New Zealand 96.00

5 **Ritz-Carlton** Berlin 96.00

8 **Oberoi Udaivilas** Udaipur, India 95.73

9 **Sabi Sabi Private Game Reserve**
Kruger National Park Area, South Africa 95.71

10 **Singita Sabi Sand** Kruger National Park
Area, South Africa 95.64

11 **Discovery Shores**
Boracay, Philippines 95.57

12 **Four Seasons Hotel Gresham Palace**
Budapest 95.52

13 **Triple Creek Ranch** Darby, Montana 95.36

14 **Jade Mountain** St. Lucia 95.33

14 **Umaid Bhawan Palace** Jodhpur, India 95.33

16 **The Lodge** Sea Island, Georgia 95.29

17 **Post Hotel & Spa**
Lake Louise, Alberta 94.93

18 **The Peninsula** Hong Kong 94.88

19 **Oberoi Rajvilas** Jaipur, India 94.84

20 **Cavas Wine Lodge**
Mendoza, Argentina 94.80

21 **Anse Chastanet Resort** St. Lucia 94.78

22 **Nisbet Plantation Beach Club** Nevis 94.67

23 **The Cloister** Sea Island, Georgia 94.63

24 **Old Edwards Inn & Spa**
Highlands, North Carolina 94.63

25 **Elizabeth Pointe Lodge**
Amelia Island, Florida 94.60

26 **Cape Grace** Cape Town 94.55

27 **La Résidence Phou Vao**
Luang Prabang, Laos 94.53

28 **The Peninsula** Beverly Hills, California 94.51

29 **Taj Lake Palace** Udaipur, India 94.50

29 **Wickaninnish Inn**
Tofino, British Columbia 94.50

31 **Mandarin Oriental** Bangkok 94.47

32 **Rosewood Mayakoba**
Riviera Maya, Mexico 94.40

33 **Stafford London by Kempinski** 94.37

34 **andBeyond Kichwa Tembo Tented Camp**
Masai Mara National Reserve, Kenya 94.35

35 **Amansara** Siem Reap, Cambodia 94.18

35 **Mandarin Oriental** Hong Kong 94.18

35 **The Peninsula** Shanghai 94.18

38 **Farmhouse Inn** Forestville, California 94.09

39 **Londolozi Game Reserve** Kruger National
Park Area, South Africa 94.08

40 **Four Seasons Hotel Cairo at Nile Plaza**
94.00

41 **Capella Pedregal** Los Cabos, Mexico 93.81

42 **Alvear Palace Hotel** Buenos Aires 93.77

43 **Dhara Dhevi** Chiang Mai, Thailand 93.76

44 **Waldorf Astoria** Chicago 93.75

45 **St. Regis Punta Mita Resort** Mexico 93.64

46 **Primland** Meadows of Dan, Virginia 93.63

47 **Four Seasons Hotel** Amman, Jordan 93.60

47 **Grand Hyatt** Istanbul 93.60

47 **Palazzo Avino** Ravello, Italy 93.60

Throughout the World's Best Awards, scores shown have
been rounded to the nearest hundredth of a point; in
the event of a true tie, properties share the same ranking.

No 1 **Hotel Overall**
MOMBO CAMP AND LITTLE MOMBO CAMP
Botswana

ᴺᴼ1 Destination Spa Overall
RANCHO LA PUERTA
Tecate, Mexico

The Top 100 Hotels (cont.)

NO.5 **Hotel Overall**
FOUR SEASONS RESORT
Bora-Bora

TOP 10 DESTINATION SPAS

1 **Rancho La Puerta Fitness Resort & Spa**
   Tecate, Mexico 94.33

2 **Ranch at Live Oak** Malibu, California 93.67

3 **Lake Austin Spa Resort** Texas 93.16

4 **Westglow Resort & Spa**
   Blowing Rock, North Carolina 93.04

5 **Miraval Resort & Spa** Tucson, Arizona 91.72

6 **Mii Amo Spa, a Destination Spa at
   Enchantment Resort** Sedona, Arizona 91.61

7 **The BodyHoliday** Castries, St. Lucia 91.57

8 **Lodge at Woodloch, a Destination Spa
   Resort** Hawley, Pennsylvania 91.08

9 **Cal-a-Vie Health Spa**
   Vista, California 90.67

10 **Sundara Inn & Spa**
   Wisconsin Dells, Wisconsin 88.22

Continental U.S.

LARGE CITY HOTELS (100 ROOMS OR MORE)

1. **The Peninsula** Beverly Hills, California 94.51
2. **Waldorf Astoria** Chicago 93.75
3. **Mandarin Oriental** Las Vegas 93.19
4. **Four Seasons Hotel** St. Louis 92.46
4. **The Peninsula** Chicago 92.46
6. **Trump International Hotel & Tower** Chicago 91.39
7. **St. Regis** New York City 91.00
8. **Ritz-Carlton, Key Biscayne, Miami** 90.83
9. **The Palazzo** Las Vegas 90.65
10. **Boston Harbor Hotel** 90.65
11. **Inn & Spa at Loretto** Santa Fe, New Mexico 90.63
12. **St. Regis** Atlanta 90.60
13. **Ritz-Carlton New York, Central Park** 90.55
14. **Four Seasons Hotel** Atlanta 90.38
15. **Ritz-Carlton** Dallas 90.37
16. **London West Hollywood** California 89.91
17. **Montage** Beverly Hills, California 89.81
18. **Hotel Monaco** Portland, Oregon 89.81
19. **Beverly Hills Hotel, Dorchester Collection** California 89.74
20. **Ritz-Carlton Chicago, a Four Seasons Hotel** 89.65
21. **Ritz-Carlton** St. Louis 89.60
22. **Raphael Hotel** Kansas City 89.57
23. **Four Seasons Hotel** New York City 89.56
24. **Hermitage Hotel** Nashville 89.52
25. **Trump International Hotel & Tower** New York City 89.46
26. **Mandarin Oriental** Miami 89.39
27. **The Hay-Adams** Washington, D.C. 89.37
28. **Four Seasons Hotel** Chicago 89.35
29. **Mandarin Oriental** New York City 89.33
30. **Four Seasons Hotel** Philadelphia 89.25
30. **Hutton Hotel** Nashville 89.25
32. **Hotel Teatro** Denver 89.23
33. **Charleston Place Hotel** South Carolina 89.11
34. **Hotel Bel-Air, Dorchester Collection** Los Angeles 89.10
35. **Rosewood Mansion on Turtle Creek** Dallas 89.08
36. **Huntington Hotel & Nob Hill Spa** San Francisco 89.06
37. **L'Ermitage** Beverly Hills, California 89.04
38. **Windsor Court Hotel** New Orleans 88.91
39. **Saint Paul Hotel** Minnesota 88.87
40. **NoMad Hotel** New York City 88.80
41. **Four Seasons Hotel** Las Vegas 88.76
42. **Four Seasons Hotel** Austin, Texas 88.72
43. **Andaz Wall Street** New York City 88.67
43. **Mandarin Oriental** San Francisco 88.67
45. **Lenox Hotel, Back Bay** Boston 88.64
46. **Four Seasons Hotel** Seattle 88.63
47. **Sofitel Chicago Water Tower** 88.62
48. **Ritz-Carlton, Buckhead** Atlanta 88.56
49. **Taj** Boston 88.47
50. **Andaz 5th Avenue** New York City 88.40

SMALL CITY HOTELS (FEWER THAN 100 ROOMS)

1. **Market Pavilion Hotel** Charleston, South Carolina 93.33
2. **Rosewood Inn of the Anasazi** Santa Fe, New Mexico 93.03
3. **Wentworth Mansion** Charleston, South Carolina 92.56
4. **French Quarter Inn** Charleston, South Carolina 90.74
5. **Fairmont Heritage Place, Ghirardelli Square** San Francisco 90.59
6. **Acqualina Resort & Spa on the Beach** Miami Beach 90.50
7. **Planters Inn** Charleston, South Carolina 90.40
8. **XV Beacon** Boston 88.75
9. **Tides South Beach** Miami Beach 88.53
10. **Arizona Inn** Tucson, Arizona 88.50

RESORTS (40 ROOMS OR MORE)

1. **The Lodge** Sea Island, Georgia 95.29
2. **The Cloister** Sea Island, Georgia 94.63
3. **Old Edwards Inn & Spa** Highlands, North Carolina 94.63
4. **Grand Del Mar** San Diego 93.27
5. **Cavallo Point—The Lodge at the Golden Gate** Sausalito, California 93.22
6. **Ritz-Carlton, Dove Mountain** Tucson, Arizona 92.77
7. **Sunset Key Guest Cottages** Key West, Florida 92.71
8. **White Elephant** Nantucket, Massachusetts 92.47
9. **Stephanie Inn** Cannon Beach, Oregon 92.26
10. **Ocean House** Watch Hill, Rhode Island 92.07
11. **Inn at Palmetto Bluff, an Auberge Resort** Bluffton, South Carolina 92.06
12. **The Sebastian** Vail, Colorado 92.00
12. **WaterColor Inn & Resort** Santa Rosa Beach, Florida 92.00
14. **Auberge du Soleil** Rutherford, California 91.87
15. **Blackberry Farm** Walland, Tennessee 91.77
16. **Marco Beach Ocean Resort** Marco Island, Florida 91.73
17. **Coeur d'Alene Golf & Spa Resort** Idaho 91.65
18. **Stowe Mountain Lodge** Stowe, Vermont 91.55
19. **Resort at Pelican Hill** Newport Beach, California 91.09
20. **Carneros Inn** Napa, California 90.93
21. **Ponte Vedra Inn & Club** Ponte Vedra Beach, Florida 90.86
22. **San Ysidro Ranch** Santa Barbara, California 90.80
23. **Inn at Spanish Bay** Pebble Beach, California 90.77
24. **Ritz-Carlton** Naples, Florida 90.74
25. **Stein Eriksen Lodge Deer Valley** Park City, Utah 90.67
26. **Ritz-Carlton, Bachelor Gulch** Avon, Colorado 90.55
27. **Sanctuary at Kiawah Island Golf Resort** South Carolina 90.52
28. **Lodge & Club at Ponte Vedra Beach** Florida 90.50
29. **Sonnenalp Hotel** Vail, Colorado 90.48
30. **Solage** Calistoga, California 90.44
31. **Little Nell** Aspen, Colorado 90.42
32. **LaPlaya Beach & Golf Resort** Naples, Florida 90.37
33. **Enchantment Resort** Sedona, Arizona 90.34
34. **L'Auberge Del Mar** Del Mar, California 90.30
35. **Osthoff Resort** Elkhart Lake, Wisconsin 90.22
36. **Ritz-Carlton** Fort Lauderdale, Florida 90.20
37. **Rancho Valencia Resort & Spa** Rancho Santa Fe, California 90.18
38. **Allison Inn & Spa** Newberg, Oregon 90.15
39. **The Breakers** Palm Beach, Florida 90.15
40. **Ritz-Carlton** Half Moon Bay, California 90.08
41. **Keswick Hall at Monticello** Keswick, Virginia 90.00
42. **Tides Inn** Irvington, Virginia 89.88
43. **Seagate Hotel & Spa** Delray Beach, Florida 89.79
44. **Calistoga Ranch** California 89.68
45. **Four Seasons Resort Scottsdale at Troon North** Arizona 89.61
46. **Willows Lodge** Woodinville, Washington 89.57
47. **Rancho Bernardo Inn Golf Resort & Spa** San Diego, California 89.46
48. **Meadowood Napa Valley** St. Helena, California 89.30
49. **Hotel Healdsburg** California 89.29
50. **Inn on Biltmore Estate** Asheville, North Carolina 89.24

Continental U.S. (cont.)

INNS AND SMALL LODGES
(FEWER THAN 40 ROOMS)

1. **Triple Creek Ranch** Darby, Montana 95.36
2. **Elizabeth Pointe Lodge**
   Amelia Island, Florida 94.60
3. **Farmhouse Inn** Forestville, California 94.09
4. **Primland** Meadows of Dan, Virginia 93.63
5. **Weekapaug Inn**
   Westerly, Rhode Island 91.60
6. **Post Ranch Inn** Big Sur, California 91.50
7. **The Willcox** Aiken, South Carolina 91.45
8. **Inn at Little Washington**
   Washington, Virginia 91.27
9. **Marquesa Hotel** Key West, Florida 90.67
9. **Tu Tu' Tun Lodge** Gold Beach, Oregon 90.67

TOP 5 HOTEL SPAS

1. **Ritz-Carlton, Bachelor Gulch**
   Avon, Colorado 97.86
2. **Mohonk Mountain House**
   Hudson Valley, New York 97.14
3. **Ocean House**
   Watch Hill, Rhode Island 97.08
4. **The Cloister** Sea Island, Georgia 96.40
5. **Grand Del Mar** San Diego 94.83

NO1 **Continental U.S. Inn**
TRIPLE CREEK RANCH
Darby, Montana

Canada

CITY HOTELS

1 **Fairmont Pacific Rim** Vancouver 92.36
2 **Ritz-Carlton** Toronto 92.00
3 **Auberge Saint-Antoine** Quebec City 90.71
4 **Shangri-La Hotel** Vancouver 90.20
5 **Wedgewood Hotel & Spa** Vancouver 89.71
6 **Fairmont Waterfront** Vancouver 89.56
7 **Auberge du Vieux-Port** Montreal 89.20
8 **Fairmont Vancouver Airport** 89.14
9 **Fairmont Château Laurier** Ottawa 88.15
10 **Fairmont Empress**
    Victoria, British Columbia 88.05

RESORTS

1 **Post Hotel & Spa** Lake Louise, Alberta 94.93
2 **Wickaninnish Inn**
   Tofino, British Columbia 94.50
3 **Four Seasons Resort**
   Whistler, British Columbia 92.74
4 **Fairmont Chateau Lake Louise**
   Alberta 89.77
5 **Fairmont Chateau Whistler**
   British Columbia 88.78
6 **Rimrock Resort Hotel**
   Banff, Alberta 88.31
7 **Fairmont Banff Springs** Alberta 85.98
8 **Westin Resort & Spa**
   Whistler, British Columbia 85.03
9 **Pillar & Post**
   Niagara-on-the-Lake, Ontario 84.00
10 **Prince of Wales Hotel**
    Niagara-on-the-Lake, Ontario 82.94

TOP HOTEL SPA

1 **Ritz-Carlton** Toronto 98.18

Hawaii

RESORTS

1 **Four Seasons Resort Hualalai**
   Hawaii, the Big Island 92.90
2 **Four Seasons Resort Maui at Wailea**
   91.73
3 **Kahala Hotel & Resort** Oahu 91.27
4 **Four Seasons Resort Lanai,**
   The Lodge at Koele 91.07
5 **St. Regis Princeville Resort** Kauai 90.43
6 **Halekulani** Oahu 90.28
7 **Royal Hawaiian, a Luxury Collection**
   Resort Oahu 90.15
8 **Fairmont Kea Lani** Maui 88.90
9 **Honua Kai Resort & Spa** Maui 88.80
10 **Mauna Kea Beach Hotel**
    Hawaii, the Big Island 87.71
11 **Koa Kea Hotel & Resort** Kauai 87.54
12 **Four Seasons Resort Lanai at**
    Manele Bay 87.08
13 **Fairmont Orchid**
    Hawaii, the Big Island 86.60
14 **Ritz-Carlton, Kapalua** Maui 86.59
15 **Travaasa Hana** Maui 86.00
16 **Mauna Lani Bay Hotel & Bungalows**
    Hawaii, the Big Island 85.66

17 **JW Marriott Ihilani Resort & Spa**
    Oahu 85.27
18 **Outrigger Waikiki on the Beach**
    Oahu 85.27
19 **Grand Hyatt Kauai Resort & Spa**
    Kauai 84.90
20 **Wailea Beach Marriott Resort & Spa**
    Maui 84.50
21 **Sheraton Kauai Resort** 84.29
22 **Sheraton Maui Resort & Spa** 83.92
23 **Hyatt Regency Waikiki Beach**
    Resort & Spa Oahu 83.70
24 **Grand Wailea Resort, a**
    Waldorf Astoria Resort Maui 83.70
25 **Embassy Suites Waikiki Beach Walk**
    Oahu 82.89

TOP 3 HOTEL SPAS

1 **Four Seasons Resort Hualalai**
   Hawaii, the Big Island 92.73
2 **St. Regis Princeville Resort** Kauai 91.50
3 **Fairmont Orchid**
   Hawaii, the Big Island 91.25

NO.1 Hawaii Resort
FOUR SEASONS RESORT HUALALAI
Hawaii, the Big Island

Mexico

The Caribbean, Bermuda + The Bahamas

Mexico (cont.)

NO 1 **Mexico Resort**
ROSEWOOD MAYAKOBA
Riviera Maya

Central+South America City Hotel
ALVEAR PALACE HOTEL
Buenos Aires

Central+South America

CITY HOTELS

1. **Alvear Palace Hotel** Buenos Aires 93.77
2. **Four Seasons Hotel** Buenos Aires 91.23
3. **Hotel Monasterio** Cuzco, Peru 91.14
4. **Sofitel Legend Santa Clara** Cartagena, Colombia 90.53
5. **Palacio Duhau–Park Hyatt** Buenos Aires 90.18
6. **JW Marriott Hotel** Quito, Ecuador 89.05
7. **Casa Andina Private Collection Miraflores** Lima, Peru 87.50
8. **Park Hyatt** Mendoza, Argentina 86.91
9. **Hotel Museo Casa Santo Domingo** Antigua, Guatemala 86.74
10. **Palacio del Inka, a Luxury Collection Hotel** Cuzco, Peru 86.67
11. **JW Marriott Lima Hotel** Peru 86.53
12. **Hotel Grano de Oro** San José, Costa Rica 85.60
13. **Ritz-Carlton** Santiago, Chile 85.37
14. **Park Tower Buenos Aires, a Luxury Collection Hotel** 85.07
15. **Grand Hyatt** Santiago, Chile 84.95

RESORTS

1. **Nayara Hotel, Spa & Gardens** La Fortuna, Costa Rica 96.14
2. **Cavas Wine Lodge** Mendoza, Argentina 94.80
3. **Four Seasons Resort Costa Rica at Peninsula Papagayo** 92.13
4. **Hotel Punta Islita** Guanacaste, Costa Rica 92.00
5. **Arenas del Mar Beachfront & Rainforest Resort** Manuel Antonio, Costa Rica 90.67
6. **Llao Llao Hotel & Resort, Golf-Spa** Bariloche, Argentina 89.88
7. **Inkaterra Machu Picchu Pueblo Hotel** Peru 89.60
8. **JW Marriott Guanacaste Resort & Spa** Costa Rica 87.29
9. **Four Seasons Resort** Carmelo, Uruguay 87.16
10. **Machu Picchu Sanctuary Lodge** Peru 86.44

TOP 3 HOTEL SPAS

1. **Nayara Hotel, Spa & Gardens** La Fortuna, Costa Rica 96.72
2. **JW Marriott Guanacaste Resort & Spa** Costa Rica 92.08
3. **Tabacón Grand Spa Thermal Resort** La Fortuna, Costa Rica 89.06

NO 2 **Central+South America Resort**

^{NO}1 **Europe Small City Hotel**
MANDARIN ORIENTAL
Munich

Europe

LARGE CITY HOTELS
(100 ROOMS OR MORE)

1 **Ritz-Carlton** Berlin 96.00
2 **Four Seasons Hotel Gresham Palace**
   Budapest 95.52
3 **Stafford London by Kempinski** 94.37
4 **Grand Hyatt** Istanbul 93.60
5 **Augustine Hotel** Prague 93.33
6 **Hotel Imperial, a Luxury Collection
   Hotel** Vienna 92.69
7 **Brenners Park-Hotel & Spa**
   Baden-Baden, Germany 92.67
8 **The Connaught, a Maybourne Hotel**
   London 92.36
9 **Corinthia Hotel** London 92.24
10 **Four Seasons Hotel George V** Paris 92.18
11 **St. Regis** Florence 91.87
12 **Hôtel Le Bristol** Paris 91.84
13 **Hotel Ritz** Madrid 91.73
14 **Four Seasons Hotel Firenze**
   Florence 91.73
15 **Mandarin Oriental Hyde Park**
   London 91.69

SMALL CITY HOTELS
(FEWER THAN 100 ROOMS)

1 **Mandarin Oriental** Munich 93.25
2 **Four Seasons Hotel Istanbul at
   Sultanahmet** 92.65
3 **Hôtel D'Europe** Avignon, France 91.85
4 **Milestone Hotel** London 91.82
5 **Hotel Cipriani** Venice 91.00
6 **Hotel Hassler Roma** Rome 90.88
7 **La Mirande** Avignon, France 90.75
8 **41** London 90.67
8 **Hotel Helvetia & Bristol** Florence 90.67
10 **Hotel Lungarno** Florence 90.31

RESORTS (40 ROOMS OR MORE)

1 **Castello di Casole—A Timbers Resort**
   Casole d'Elsa, Italy 96.18
2 **Palazzo Avino (formerly Palazzo Sasso)**
   Ravello, Italy 93.60
3 **Ashford Castle** County Mayo, Ireland 93.17
4 **Hotel Santa Caterina** Amalfi, Italy 92.74
5 **Le Sirenuse** Positano, Italy 92.31
6 **Il San Pietro di Positano** Italy 92.28
7 **Grand Hotel Excelsior Vittoria**
   Sorrento, Italy 91.45
8 **Villa d'Este** Cernobbio, Italy 90.39
9 **Grand Hotel Quisisana** Capri, Italy 89.76
10 **Dromoland Castle Hotel**
   County Clare, Ireland 89.50

INNS AND SMALL LODGES
(FEWER THAN 40 ROOMS)

1 **Domaine Les Crayères**
   Reims, France 93.24
2 **Hôtel Crillon le Brave**
   Crillon-le-Brave, France 90.53
3 **Oustau de Baumanière & Spa**
   Les Baux-de-Provence, France 90.00
4 **Château Eza** Eze Village, France 89.88
5 **La Chèvre d'Or** Eze Village, France 89.47
6 **Cliveden House** Taplow, England 89.33
7 **Villa Gallici** Aix-en-Provence, France 89.22
8 **Waterford Castle** Waterford, Ireland 88.94
9 **Le Manoir aux Quat'Saisons**
   Great Milton, England 88.27
10 **Hotel Villa Cipriani** Asolo, Italy 87.78

TOP 5 HOTEL SPAS

1 **Four Seasons Hotel Istanbul at the
   Bosphorus** 93.64
2 **Four Seasons Hotel George V**
   Paris 93.26
3 **Four Seasons Hotel Firenze**
   Florence 92.92
4 **Rome Cavalieri, Waldorf Astoria
   Hotels & Resorts** 92.81
5 **Hotel Grande Bretagne, a Luxury
   Collection Hotel** Athens 92.00

NO 1 **Europe Inn**
DOMAINE LES CRAYÈRES
Reims, France

Africa + The Middle East Lodge
SINGITA SABI SAND
South Africa

Africa+The Middle East

CITY HOTELS

1. **Cape Grace** Cape Town 94.55
2. **Four Seasons Hotel Cairo at Nile Plaza** 94.00
3. **Four Seasons Hotel** Amman, Jordan 93.60
4. **Saxon Hotel, Villas & Spa** Johannesburg, South Africa 93.50
5. **Four Seasons Hotel Cairo at the First Residence** 92.53
6. **Mount Nelson Hotel** Cape Town 91.50
7. **Burj Al Arab** Dubai 90.51
8. **La Mamounia** Marrakesh, Morocco 90.29
9. **Mena House Oberoi** Cairo 90.24
10. **Twelve Apostles Hotel & Spa** Cape Town 89.48
11. **One&Only** Cape Town 88.67
12. **King David Hotel** Jerusalem 87.93
13. **Victoria & Alfred Hotel** Cape Town 87.48
14. **Westcliff Hotel** Johannesburg, South Africa 87.03
15. **David InterContinental** Tel Aviv 85.14

LODGES AND RESORTS

1. **Mombo Camp and Little Mombo Camp** Moremi Game Reserve, Botswana 96.60
2. **Singita Kruger National Park** South Africa 96.14
3. **Sabi Sabi Private Game Reserve** Kruger National Park Area, South Africa 95.71
4. **Singita Sabi Sand** Kruger National Park Area, South Africa 95.64
5. **andBeyond Kichwa Tembo Tented Camp** Masai Mara National Reserve, Kenya 94.35
6. **Londolozi Game Reserve** Kruger National Park Area, South Africa 94.08
7. **MalaMala Game Reserve** Kruger National Park Area, South Africa 91.53
8. **Fairmont Mount Kenya Safari Club** Nanyuki, Kenya 91.23
9. **Fairmont Mara Safari Club** Masai Mara National Reserve, Kenya 91.20
10. **andBeyond Ngorongoro Crater Lodge** Tanzania 91.11
11. **Tortilis Camp** Amboseli National Park, Kenya 91.00
12. **Royal Livingstone** Victoria Falls, Zambia 90.80
13. **Giraffe Manor** Nairobi, Kenya 90.13
14. **Le Quartier Français** Franschhoek, South Africa 89.23
15. **Ngorongoro Sopa Lodge** Tanzania 89.09
16. **Gibb's Farm** Karatu, Tanzania 89.07
17. **Amboseli Serena Safari Lodge** Amboseli National Park, Kenya 88.96
18. **Serengeti Serena Safari Lodge** Serengeti National Park, Tanzania 88.71
19. **Chobe Game Lodge** Chobe National Park, Botswana 87.17
20. **Arusha Coffee Lodge** Tanzania 84.32

TOP HOTEL SPA

1. **One&Only** Cape Town 85.36

world's best awards

253

ᴺᴼ1 Asia City Hotel

THE PENINSULA
Hong Kong

Asia

CITY HOTELS

1 **The Peninsula** Hong Kong 94.88

2 **Mandarin Oriental** Bangkok 94.47

3 **Mandarin Oriental** Hong Kong 94.18

3 **The Peninsula** Shanghai 94.18

5 **Sofitel Legend Metropole**
Hanoi, Vietnam 93.33

5 **The Oberoi** Gurgaon, India 93.33

7 **The Peninsula** Tokyo 93.11

8 **Taj Mahal Palace** Mumbai 93.02

9 **Ritz-Carlton Beijing,
Financial Street** 93.00

10 **The Peninsula** Bangkok 92.87

11 **The Oberoi** Mumbai 92.71

12 **Fullerton Bay Hotel** Singapore 92.44

13 **Island Shangri-La** Hong Kong 91.47

14 **JW Marriott Hotel** Bangkok 91.29

15 **Shangri-La Hotel** Beijing 91.24

16 **La Résidence d'Angkor**
Siem Reap, Cambodia 91.17

17 **Park Hyatt Saigon**
Ho Chi Minh City, Vietnam 91.13

18 **Shangri-La Hotel** Bangkok 91.12

19 **St. Regis Hotel** Singapore 91.11

20 **The Langham** Hong Kong 91.06

21 **The Peninsula** Beijing 90.79

22 **Pudong Shangri-La East Shanghai**
90.71

23 **St. Regis** Beijing 90.67

24 **Park Hyatt** Shanghai 90.53

25 **Ritz-Carlton** Tokyo 90.40

26 **Four Seasons Hotel** Bangkok 90.36

27 **JW Marriott Hotel Shanghai
at Tomorrow Square** 90.29

28 **Regent** Beijing 90.25

29 **Westin Bund Center** Shanghai 90.20

30 **Four Seasons Hotel** Hong Kong 90.13

RESORTS

1 **Oberoi Udaivilas** Udaipur, India 95.73

2 **Discovery Shores**
Boracay, Philippines 95.57

3 **Umaid Bhawan Palace**
Jodhpur, India 95.33

4 **Oberoi Rajvilas** Jaipur, India 94.84

5 **La Résidence Phou Vao**
Luang Prabang, Laos 94.53

6 **Taj Lake Palace** Udaipur, India 94.50

7 **Amansara** Siem Reap, Cambodia 94.18

8 **Dhara Dhevi** Chiang Mai, Thailand 93.76

9 **Oberoi Amarvilas** Agra, India 93.44

10 **Sofitel Angkor Phokeethra Golf & Spa**
Siem Reap, Cambodia 92.57

11 **Rambagh Palace** Jaipur, India 91.76

12 **Nam Hai** Hoi An, Vietnam 91.71

13 **Four Seasons Resort**
Chiang Mai, Thailand 91.59

14 **Raffles Grand Hotel d'Angkor**
Siem Reap, Cambodia 90.67

15 **Shangri-La Boracay Resort & Spa**
Boracay, Philippines 89.92

TOP 5 HOTEL SPAS

1 **Discovery Shores**
Boracay, Philippines 97.83

2 **Nam Hai** Hoi An, Vietnam 97.81

3 **Sofitel Legend Metropole**
Hanoi, Vietnam 97.50

4 **Anantara Golden Triangle Elephant
Camp & Resort** Chiang Rai, Thailand 96.00

5 **Four Seasons Resort**
Chiang Mai, Thailand 95.00

Australia, New Zealand + The South Pacific

CITY HOTELS

1. **The Langham** Melbourne, Australia 89.60
2. **Shangri-La Hotel** Sydney 88.36
3. **InterContinental** Sydney 88.22
4. **Park Hyatt** Sydney 88.15
5. **Four Seasons Hotel** Sydney 85.72
6. **Sydney Harbour Marriott Hotel** Sydney 85.60
7. **The George** Christchurch, New Zealand 85.00
8. **Hilton** Auckland, New Zealand 83.13
9. **Sheraton on the Park** Sydney 82.62
10. **Park Hyatt** Melbourne 82.31

3. **Huka Lodge** Taupo, New Zealand 93.07
4. **St. Regis Bora Bora Resort** French Polynesia 91.61
5. **Hayman** Great Barrier Reef, Australia 91.11
6. **Hilton Bora Bora Nui Resort & Spa** French Polynesia 84.27
7. **Hilton Moorea Lagoon Resort & Spa** French Polynesia 83.37
8. **Shangri-La Hotel, The Marina** Cairns, Australia 82.67
9. **InterContinental Tahiti Resort** French Polynesia 78.71
10. **Le Méridien** Tahiti, French Polynesia 74.00

RESORTS

1. **Four Seasons Resort** Bora-Bora, French Polynesia 96.00
1. **Lodge at Kauri Cliffs** New Zealand 96.00

TOP HOTEL SPA

1. **St. Regis Bora Bora** French Polynesia 89.09

Australia, New Zealand + The South Pacific City Hotel

PARK HYATT
Sydney

A reflecting pool
at the Oberoi,
Gurgaon, near
New Delhi.

T+L 500

United States

Arizona

PHOENIX/SCOTTSDALE

Four Seasons Resort Scottsdale at Troon North 89.61
10600 E. Crescent Moon Dr., Scottsdale; 800/332-3442; fourseasons.com. **$$$**

Hermosa Inn 90.35
5532 N. Palo Cristi Rd., Paradise Valley; 800/241-1210; hermosainn.com. **$$$**

JW Marriott Camelback Inn Resort & Spa 87.92
5402 E. Lincoln Dr., Scottsdale; 800/228-9290; jwmarriott.com. **$$$**

Omni Scottsdale Resort & Spa at Montelucia (formerly the Montelucia Resort & Spa) 88.86
4949 E. Lincoln Dr., Scottsdale; 800/943-6664; omnihotels.com. **$$**

The Phoenician, a Luxury Collection Resort 88.95
6000 E. Cambelback Rd., Scottsdale; 800/325-3589; thephoenician.com. **$$$$**

Royal Palms Resort & Spa 89.05
5200 E. Camelback Rd., Phoenix; 800/672-6011; royalpalmsresortandspa.com. **$$$**

Sanctuary on Camelback Mountain 88.77
5700 E. McDonald Dr., Paradise Valley; 800/245-2051; santuaryaz.com. **$$$**

SEDONA

Enchantment Resort & Mii amo Spa 90.34
888/749-2137; enchantmentresort.com. **$$$**

L'Auberge de Sedona 88.00
800/905-5745; lauberge.com. **$$**

TUCSON

Arizona Inn 88.50
2200 E. Elm St.; 800/933-1093; arizonainn.com. **$$**

Ritz-Carlton, Dove Mountain 92.77
15000 N. Secret Springs Dr.; 800/241-3333; ritzcarlton.com. **$$**

California

BIG SUR

Post Ranch Inn 91.50
888/524-4787; postranchinn.com. **$$$$**

CARLSBAD

Four Seasons Residence Club Aviara 87.59
800/332-3442; fourseasons.com. **$$$**

CARMEL

L'Auberge Carmel 88.00
800/735-2478; laubergecarmel.com. **$$$**

DEL MAR

L'Auberge Del Mar 90.30
800/245-9757; laubergedelmar.com. **$$$**

HALF MOON BAY

Ritz-Carlton 90.08
800/241-3333; ritzcarlton.com. **$$$**

LOS ANGELES

Beverly Hills Hotel, Dorchester Collection 89.74
9641 Sunset Blvd., Beverly Hills; 800/650-1842; beverlyhillshotel.com. **$$$**

Four Seasons Hotel Los Angeles at Beverly Hills 88.00
300 S. Doheny Dr., Los Angeles; 800/332-3442; fourseasons.com. **$$$**

Hotel Bel-Air, Dorchester Collection 89.10
701 Stone Canyon Rd., Los Angeles; 800/650-1842; hotelbelair.com. **$$$**

L'Ermitage Beverly Hills 89.04
9291 Burton Way, Beverly Hills; 877/235-7582; lermitagebh.com. **$$$**

London West Hollywood 89.91
1020 N. San Vicente Blvd., West Hollywood; 866/282-4560; thelondonwesthollywood.com. **$$$**

Montage Beverly Hills 89.82
225 N. Canon Dr., Beverly Hills; 888/860-0788; montagebeverlyhills.com. **$$$$**

Peninsula Beverly Hills 94.51
9882 S. Santa Monica Blvd., Beverly Hills; 866/382-8388; peninsula.com. **$$$$**

NAPA/SONOMA

Auberge de Soleil 91.87
Rutherford; 800/348-5406; aubergedusoleil.com. **$$$$**

Calistoga Ranch 89.68
Calistoga; 855/942-4220; calistogaranch.com. **$$$$**

Carneros Inn 90.93
Napa; 888/400-9000; thecarnerosinn.com. **$$$$**

Farmhouse Inn 94.09
Forestville; 800/464-6642; farmhouseinn.com. **$$$**

Hotel Healdsburg 89.29
Healdsburg; 800/889-7188; hotelhealdsburg.com. **$$$**

Meadowood Napa Valley 89.30
St. Helena; 877/686-5197; meadowood.com. **$$$$**

Solage Calistoga 90.44
Calistoga; 855/942-7442; solagecalistoga.com. **$$$**

Villagio Inn & Spa 88.24
Yountville; 800/351-1133; villagio.com. **$$$**

Vintage Inn 88.37
Yountville; 800/351-1133; vintageinn.com. **$$$**

ORANGE COUNTY

Montage Laguna Beach 88.55
Laguna Beach; 866/271-6951; montagelagunabeach.com. **$$$$**

Resort at Pelican Hill 91.09
Newport Coast; 855/467-6800; pelicanhill.com. **$$$**

St. Regis Monarch Beach 89.02
Dana Point; 877/787-3447; stregis.com. **$$$$**

PEBBLE BEACH

Inn at Spanish Bay 90.77
800/654-9300; pebblebeach.com. **$$$$**

Lodge at Pebble Beach 88.75
800/654-9300; pebblebeach.com. **$$$$**

RANCHO PALOS VERDES

Terranea 89.16
866/802-8000; terranea.com. **$$$**

RANCHO SANTA FE

Rancho Valencia Resort & Spa 90.18
866/233-6708; ranchovalencia.com. **$$$$**

SAN DIEGO

Grand Del Mar 93.27
5300 Grand Del Mar Court; 877/814-8472; thegranddelmar.com. **$$$**

Ⓢ **Rancho Bernardo Inn Golf Resort & Spa** 89.46
17550 Bernardo Oaks Dr.; 877/517-9340; ranchobernardoinn.com. **$$**

SAN FRANCISCO AREA

Cavallo Point—The Lodge at the Golden Gate 93.22
Sausalito; 888/651-2003; cavallopoint.com. **$$$**

Fairmont Heritage Place, Ghirardelli Square 90.59
900 N. Point St., San Francisco; 800/441-1414; fairmont.com. **$$$**

Huntington Hotel & Nob Hill Spa 89.06
1075 California St., San Francisco; 800/227-4683; huntingtonhotel.com. **$$$**

Mandarin Oriental 88.67
222 Sansome St., San Francisco; 800/526-6566; mandarinoriental.com. **$$$$**

Ⓢ **Taj Campton Place** 88.33
340 Stockton St., San Francisco; 866/969-1825; tajhotels.com. **$$**

SAN JOSE

Hotel Valencia Santana Row 88.00
355 Santana Row; 866/842-0100; hotelvalencia-santanarow.com. **$$**

SANTA BARBARA AREA

Canary Hotel, a Kimpton Hotel 87.67
31 W. Carrillo St., Santa Barbara; 800/546-7866; kimptonhotels.com. **$$$**

Four Seasons Resort The Biltmore 87.87
Montecito; 800/332-2442; fourseasons.com. **$$$**

San Ysidro Ranch 90.80
Montecito; 800/368-6788; sanysidroranch.com. **$$$**

SANTA MONICA

Shutters on the Beach 87.80
1 Pico Blvd.; 800/334-9000; shuttersonthebeach.com. **$$$$**

VENTURA

Ojai Valley Inn & Spa 88.47
855/217-9065; ojairesort.com. **$$$**

Colorado

ASPEN

Little Nell 90.42
855/920-4600; thelittlenell.com. **$$$$**

Ritz-Carlton, Bachelor Gulch 90.55
800/241-3333; ritzcarlton.com. **$$$$**

BEAVER CREEK

Beaver Creek Lodge 88.17
800/583-9615; beavercreeklodge.net. **$$$**

Pines Lodge, a RockResort 88.22
855/279-3430; rockresorts.com. **$$**

COLORADO SPRINGS

The Broadmoor 88.88
800/634-7711; broadmoor.com. **$$$**

DENVER

Hotel Teatro 89.23
1100 14th St.; 888/727-1200; hotelteatro.com. **$$**

Ritz-Carlton, Denver 87.59
1881 Curtis St.; 800/241-3333; ritzcarlton.com. **$$**

VAIL

The Sebastian 92.00
800/354-6908; thesebastianvail.com. **$$**

Sonnenalp Hotel 90.48
800/654-8312; sonnenalp.com. **$$$$**

Connecticut

WASHINGTON

Mayflower Grace 87.65
860/868-9466; gracehotels.com. **$$$$**

District of Columbia

WASHINGTON, D.C.

Four Seasons Hotel 88.00
2800 Pennsylvania Ave. NW; 800/332-3442; fourseasons.com. **$$$**

The Hay-Adams 89.37
16th St. NW; 800/424-5054; hayadams.com. **$$**

Lounge chairs by the pool area at the Farmhouse Inn, in California.

Ritz-Carlton Georgetown
88.44
3100 South St. NW;
800/241-3333;
ritzcarlton.com. $$$$

Florida
AMELIA ISLAND
🅢 **Elizabeth Pointe Lodge**
94.60
800/772-3359;
elizabethpointelodge.com. $$

Ritz-Carlton 88.98
800/241-3333;
ritzcarlton.com. $$$

BAL HARBOUR
**St. Regis Bal Harbour
Resort** 88.14
877/787-3447; *stregis.com.*
$$$$

CLEARWATER BEACH
Sandpearl Resort 88.19
877/726-3111;
sandpearl.com. $$$

DELRAY BEACH
Seagate Hotel & Spa 89.79
877/577-3242;
theseagatehotel.com. $$

FLORIDA KEYS
Little Palm Island

Resort & Spa 90.16
Little Torch Key; 800/343-
8567; *littlepalmisland.com.*
$$$$

Marquesa Hotel 90.67
Key West; 800/869-4631;
marquesa.com. $$

**Sunset Key Guest
Cottages, a Westin Resort**
92.71
Key West; 800/228-3000;
westinsunsetkeycottages.com.
$$$$$

FORT LAUDERDALE
Ritz-Carlton 90.20
866/241-3333;
ritzcarlton.com. $$$$

JACKSONVILLE AREA
**Lodge & Club at Ponte
Vedra Beach** 90.50
Ponte Vedra Beach;
800/243-4304;
pontevedra.com. $$

Ponte Vedra Inn & Club
90.86
Ponte Vedra Beach; 800/234-
7842; *pontevedra.com.* $$

MARCO ISLAND
Marco Beach Ocean

Resort 91.73
800/715-8517;
marcoresort.com. $$$

MIAMI AREA
**Acqualina Resort & Spa on
the Beach** 90.50
17875 Collins Ave., Sunny
Isles Beach; 877/765-1242;
acqualina.com. $$$$

Four Seasons Hotel 87.79
1435 Brickell Ave., Miami;
800/332-3442;
fourseasons.com. $$$

Mandarin Oriental 89.39
500 Brickell Key Dr., Miami;
800/526-6566;
mandarinoriental.com. $$$$

Ritz-Carlton Key Biscayne
90.29
455 Grand Bay Dr., Miami;
800/241-3333;
ritzcarlton.com. $$$$

Ritz-Carlton South Beach
87.61
1 Lincoln Rd., Miami Beach;
800/241-3333;
ritzcarlton.com. $$$

Tides South Beach 88.53
1220 Ocean Dr., Miami Beach;

866/438-4337;
tidessouthbeach.com. $$$

NAPLES
**LaPlaya Beach &
Golf Resort** 90.37
800/237-6883;
laplayaresort.com. $$$$

Ritz-Carlton 90.74
800/241-3333;
ritzcarlton.com. $$$$$

Ritz-Carlton Golf Resort
88.82
800/241-3333;
ritzcarlton.com. $$$$

ORLANDO AREA
**Disney's Grand Floridian
Resort & Spa** 88.00
Lake Buena Vista;
407/939-3476;
disneyworld.com. $$$$

PALM BEACH
Brazilian Court Hotel 88.87
800/552-0335;
thebraziliancourt.com. $$$$

The Breakers 90.15
888/273-2537;
thebreakers.com. $$$$

**Eau Palm Beach Resort
(formerly the Ritz-Carlton
Palm Beach)** 88.00
800/328-0170;
eaupalmbeach.com. $$$$

SANTA ROSA BEACH
WaterColor Inn & Resort
92.00
866/426-2656;
watercolorresort.com. $$$

SARASOTA
**Resort at Longboat Key
Club** 88.14
800/237-8821;
longboatkeyclub.com. $$$

ST. PETERSBURG
**Renaissance Vinoy Resort
& Golf Club** 88.20
888/303-4430;
marriott.com. $$

Georgia
ATLANTA
Four Seasons Hotel 90.38
75 14th St. N.W.; 800/332-
3442; *fourseasons.com.* $$$

Ritz-Carlton, Buckhead
88.56
3434 Peachtree Rd. N.E.;
800/241-3333;
ritzcarlton.com. $$$$

St. Regis 90.60
88. W. Paces Ferry Rd.;

877/787-3447; *stregis.com.*
$$$$

SAVANNAH
🅢 **Bohemian Hotel
Savannah Riverfront** 87.88
102 W. Bay St.; 888/213-
4024; *bohemianhotel
savannah.com.* $$

SEA ISLAND
The Cloister 94.63
855/714-9201;
seaisland.com. $$$

The Lodge 95.29
855/714-9201;
seaisland.com. $$$

Hawaii
BIG ISLAND
**Four Seasons Resort
Hualalai** 92.90
800/332-3442;
fourseasons.com. $$$$

Mauna Kea Beach Hotel
87.71
866/977-4589;
maunakeabeachhotel.com.
$$$$

KAUAI
**St. Regis Princeville
Resort** 90.43
877/787-3447; *stregis.com.*
$$$$

LANAI
**Four Seasons Resort
Lanai, The Lodge at Koele**
91.07
800/332-3442;
fourseasons.com. $$

MAUI
Fairmont Kea Lani 88.90
800/441-1414;
fairmont.com. $$$$

**Four Seasons Resort Maui
at Wailea** 91.73
800/332-3442;
fourseasons.com. $$$

Honua Kai Resort & Spa
88.80
888/718-5789;
honuakai.com. $$

OAHU
Halekulani 90.28
800/367-2343;
halekulani.com. $$$

Kahala Hotel & Resort
91.27
800/367-2525;
kahalaresort.com. $$$

**Royal Hawaiian, a Luxury
Collection Resort** 90.15
800/325-3589;
royal-hawaiian.com. $$$$

The front entrance to XV Beacon, in Boston.

Idaho

COEUR D'ALENE

Ⓢ **Coeur d'Alene Resort** 91.65
800/688-5253; *cdaresort.com.* **$**

Illinois

CHICAGO

Ⓢ **The Blackstone** 88.36
636 S. Michigan Ave.;
888/718-5789; *blackstonerenaissance.com.* **$**

Four Seasons Hotel 89.35
120 E. Delaware Place;
800/332-3442; *fourseasons.com.* **$$**

Peninsula Chicago 92.46
108 E. Superior St.;
866/382-8388; *peninsula.com.* **$$$$**

Ritz-Carlton Chicago, a Four Seasons Hotel 89.65
160 E. Pearson St.;
800/332-3442; *fourseasons.com.* **$$**

Ⓢ **Sofitel Chicago Water Tower** 88.62
20 E. Chestnut St.; 800/
763-4835; *sofitel.com.* **$**

Trump International Hotel & Tower 91.39
401 N. Wabash Ave.;
877/458-7867; *trumpchicagohotel.com.* **$$$**

Waldorf Astoria 93.75
11 E. Walton St.; 800/925-3673; *waldorfastoria.com.* **$$**

Louisiana

NEW ORLEANS

Windsor Court Hotel 88.91
300 Gravier St.;
800/262-2662; *windsorcourthotel.com.* **$$$**

Massachusetts

BOSTON

Boston Harbor Hotel 90.65
70 Rowes Wharf; 800/752-7077; *bhh.com.* **$$$**

Four Seasons Hotel 88.15
200 Boylston St.;
800/332-3442; *fourseasons.com.* **$$$$**

The Lenox 88.64
61 Exeter St.; 800/225-7676; *lenoxhotel.com.* **$$**

Mandarin Oriental 88.32
776 Boylston St.; 800/526-6566; *mandarinoriental.com.* **$$$$**

Taj Boston 88.47
15 Arlington St.; 877/482-5267; *tajhotels.com.* **$$$**

XV Beacon 88.75
15 Beacon St.; 877/982-3226; *xvbeacon.com.* **$$$$**

NANTUCKET

The Wauwinet 89.07
800/426-8718; *wauwinet.com.* **$$$$**

White Elephant 92.47
800/445-6574; *whiteelephanthotel.com.* **$$$$**

Michigan

BAY HARBOR

Inn at Bay Harbor 88.00
800/462-6963; *innatbayharbor.com.* **$$**

GRAND RAPIDS

Ⓢ **Amway Grand Plaza Hotel** 88.00
800/253-3590; *amwaygrand.com.* **$**

MACKINAC ISLAND

Grand Hotel 88.19
800/334-7263; *grandhotel.com.* **$$**

Minnesota

ST. PAUL

Ⓢ **Saint Paul Hotel** 88.87
350 Market St.; 800/292-9292; *saintpaulhotel.com.* **$**

Missouri

KANSAS CITY

Ⓢ **Raphael Hotel** 89.57
325 Ward Pkwy.; 800/821-5342; *raphaelkc.com.* **$**

ST. LOUIS

Four Seasons Hotel 92.46
999 N. 2nd St.; 800/332-3442; *fourseasons.com.* **$$$**

Ritz-Carlton 89.60
100 Carondelet Plaza;
800/241-3333; *ritzcarlton.com.* **$$**

Montana

DARBY

Triple Creek Ranch 95.36
800/654-2943; *triplecreekranch.com.* **$$$$**

Nevada

LAS VEGAS

Bellagio Resort & Casino 88.17
3600 Las Vegas Blvd. S.;
888/987-6667; *bellagio.com.* **$$**

Four Seasons Hotel 88.76
3960 Las Vegas Blvd. S.;

800/332-3442; *fourseasons.com.* **$$**

Ⓢ **Mandarin Oriental** 93.19
3752 Las Vegas Blvd. S.;
800/526-6566; *mandarinoriental.com.* **$$**

The Palazzo 90.65
3325 Las Vegas Blvd. S.;
866/263-3001; *palazzolasvegas.com.* **$$**

Ⓢ **Wynn Las Vegas** 88.33
3131 Las Vegas Blvd. S.;
888/320-9966; *wynnlasvegas.com.* **$**

New Hampshire

JACKSON

Ⓢ **Inn at Thorn Hill & Spa** 88.80
800/289-8990; *innatthornhill.com.* **$**

New Mexico

SANTA FE

Ⓢ **Inn & Spa at Loretto** 90.63
800/727-5531; *innatloretto.com.* **$**

Rosewood Inn of the Anasazi 93.03
888/767-3966; *innoftheanasazi.com.* **$$**

New York

COOPERSTOWN

Otesaga Resort Hotel 88.20
800/348-6222; *otesaga.com.* **$$$$**

NEW PALTZ

Mohonk Mountain House 88.00
877/684-1021; *mohonk.com;* all-inclusive. **$$$$**

NEW YORK CITY

Andaz 5th Avenue 88.40
485 5th Ave.; 877/875-5036; *andaz.com.* **$$**

Ⓢ **Andaz Wall Street** 88.67
75 Wall St.; 877/875-5036; *andaz.com.* **$$**

Four Seasons Hotel 89.56
57 E. 57th St.; 800/332-3442; *fourseasons.com.* **$$$$**

Mandarin Oriental 89.33
80 Columbus Circle;
800/526-6566; *mandarinoriental.com.* **$$$$**

NoMad Hotel 88.80
1170 Broadway; 855/796-1505; *thenomadhotel.com.* **$$**

The Pierre 88.35
2 E. 61st St.; 866/969-1825; *tajhotels.com.* **$$$**

The Plaza 88.09
Fifth Ave. at Central Park S.;
888/850-0909; *theplazany.com.* **$$$$**

Ritz-Carlton New York, Battery Park 88.13
2 West St.; 800/241-3333; *ritzcarlton.com.* **$$$$**

Ritz-Carlton New York, Central Park 90.56
50 Central Park S.;
800/241-3333; *ritzcarlton.com.* **$$$$**

St. Regis 91.00
2 E. 55th St.; 877/787-3447; *stregis.com.* **$$$$**

Trump International Hotel & Tower 89.46
1 Central Park W.; 855/878-6700; *trumpintl.com.* **$$$$**

North Carolina

ASHEVILLE

Grand Bohemian Hotel 88.35
888/717-8756; *bohemian hotelasheville.com.* **$$**

Inn on Biltmore Estate 89.24
800/411-3812; *biltmore.com.* **$$$**

HIGHLANDS

Old Edwards Inn & Spa 94.63
866/526-8008; *oldedwardsinn.com.* **$$**

PITTSBORO

Fearrington House Inn, Restaurant & Spa 87.56
919/542-2121; *fearrington.com.* **$$**

Oregon

CANNON BEACH

Stephanie Inn Hotel 92.26
800/633-3466; *stephanieinn.com.* **$$$$**

GOLD BEACH

Tu Tu' Tun Lodge 90.67
800/864-6357; *tututun.com.* **$$**

NEWBERG

Allison Inn & Spa 90.15
877/294-2525; *theallison.com.* **$$$**

PORTLAND

Ⓢ **Hotel Monaco** 89.81
506 S.W. Washington St.;

888/207-2201; *monaco-portland.com.* **$$**

Pennsylvania

BEDFORD

Omni Bedford Springs Resort 88.77
814/623-8100; *omnihotels.com.* **$$**

HERSHEY

Hotel Hershey 87.85
800/437-7439; *thehotelhershey.com.* **$$**

PHILADELPHIA

Four Seasons Hotel 89.25
1 Logan Square; 800/332-3442; *fourseasons.com.* **$$**

Rittenhouse 88.00
210 W. Rittenhouse Square;
800/635-1042; *rittenhousehotel.com.* **$$$**

Ritz-Carlton 88.32
10 Ave. of the Arts;
800/241-3333; *ritzcarlton.com.* **$$**

Rhode Island

NEWPORT

Chanler at Cliff Walk 89.00
866/793-5664; *thechanler.com.* **$$$$**

WATCH HILL

Ocean House 92.07
888/552-2588; *oceanhouseri.com.* **$$$$**

WESTERLY

Weekapaug Inn 91.60
888/813-7862; *weekapauginn.com.* **$$$**

South Carolina

AIKEN

Ⓢ **The Willcox** 91.45
877/648-2200; *thewillcox.com.* **$$**

BLUFFTON

Inn at Palmetto Bluff, an Auberge Resort 92.06
800/501-7405; *palmettobluff.com.* **$$$**

CHARLESTON

Charleston Place 89.11
205 Meeting St.;
888/635-2350; *charlestonplace.com.* **$$**

Ⓢ **French Quarter Inn** 90.74
166 Church St.; 866/812-1900; *fqicharleston.com.* **$**

Market Pavilion Hotel 93.33
225 E. Bay St.; 843/723-0500; *marketpavilion.com.* **$$**

Planters Inn 90.40
112 N. Market St.;
800/845-7082;
plantersinn.com. **$$$**

Wentworth Mansion 92.56
149 Wentworth St.; 888/466-1886; *wentworth mansion.com.* **$$$**

KIAWAH ISLAND
Sanctuary at Kiawah Island Golf Resort 90.52
800/654-2924;
kiawahresort.com. **$$$**

Tennessee
NASHVILLE
Hermitage Hotel 89.52
231 6th Ave. N.;
888/888-9414;
thehermitagehotel.com. **$$**

Hutton Hotel 89.25
1808 West End Ave.;
866/894-4609;
huttonhotel.com. **$$**

WALLAND
Blackberry Farm 91.77
800/557-8864;
blackberryfarm.com. **$$$$**

Texas
AUSTIN
The Driskill 87.92
604 Brazos St.; 800/233-1234; *driskillhotel.com.* **$$**

Four Seasons Hotel 88.72
98 San Jacinto Blvd.;
800/332-3442;
fourseasons.com. **$$$**

DALLAS
Ritz-Carlton 90.37
2121 McKinney Ave.;
800/241-3333;
ritzcarlton.com. **$$$**

Rosewood Mansion on Turtle Creek 89.08
2821 Turtle Creek Blvd.;
888/767-3966; *mansion onturtlecreek.com.* **$$$**

SAN ANTONIO
Hyatt Regency Hill Country Resort & Spa 88.15
9800 Hyatt Resort Dr.; 800/223-1234; *hyatt.com.* **$$**

Utah
PARK CITY
Stein Eriksen Lodge 90.67
800/453-1302;
steinlodge.com. **$$$$**

Vermont
STOWE
Stowe Mountain Lodge 91.55
888/478-6938;
stowemountainlodge.com. **$$**

WOODSTOCK
Woodstock Inn & Resort 87.74
800/448-7900;
woodstockinn.com. **$$$**

Virginia
ARLINGTON
Ⓢ **Ritz-Carlton, Pentagon City** 87.89
800/241-3333;
ritzcarlton.com. **$**

IRVINGTON
Ⓢ **Tides Inn** 89.88
800/843-3746;
tidesinn.com. **$**

KESWICK
Keswick Hall at Monticello 90.00
800/274-5391;
keswick.com. **$$$**

MEADOWS OF DAN
Primland 93.63
866/960-7746;
primland.com. **$$**

WASHINGTON
Inn at Little Washington 91.27
540/675-3800; *theinnatlittle washington.com.* **$$$$**

Washington
KIRKLAND
Ⓢ **Woodmark Hotel, Yacht Club & Spa** 89.00
800/822-3700;
thewoodmark.com. **$**

SEATTLE
Fairmont Olympic Hotel 87.93
411 University St.; 888/363-5022; *fairmont.com.* **$$$**

Four Seasons Hotel 88.63
99 Union St.; 800/332-3442;
fourseasons.com. **$$$**

WOODINVILLE
Willows Lodge 89.57
877/424-3930;
willowslodge.com. **$$**

West Virginia
WHITE SULPHUR SPRINGS
Ⓢ **The Greenbrier** 88.71
800/624-6070;
greenbrier.com. **$$**

Wisconsin
ELKHART LAKE
Ⓢ **Osthoff Resort** 90.22
800/876-3399;
osthoff.com. **$$**

KOHLER
American Club Resort 87.59
800/344-2838;
americanclubresort.com. **$$**

Wyoming
TETON VILLAGE
Four Seasons Resort & Residences Jackson Hole 89.11
800/332-3442;
fourseasons.com. **$$$$**

Canada
Alberta
BANFF
Rimrock Resort Hotel 88.31
888/746-7625;
rimrockresort.com. **$$**

LAKE LOUISE
Fairmont Chateau Lake Louise 89.77
800/441-1414; *fairmont.com.* **$$$**

Post Hotel & Spa 94.93
800/661-1586;
posthotel.com. **$$**

British Columbia
TOFINO
Wickaninnish Inn 94.50
800/333-4604; *wickinn.com.* **$$$$**

VANCOUVER
Ⓢ **Fairmont Pacific Rim** 92.36
1038 Canada Place;
800/441-1414;
fairmont.com. **$$**

Fairmont Vancouver Airport 89.14
3111 Grant McConachie Way;
866/540-4441;
fairmont.com. **$$**

Ⓢ **Fairmont Waterfront** 89.56
900 Canada Place Way;
866/540-4509;
fairmont.com. **$**

Four Seasons Hotel 87.92
791 W. Georgia St.; 800/332-3442; *fourseasons.com.* **$$$**

Shangri-La Hotel 90.20
1128 W. Georgia St.;
866/565-5050;
shangri-la.com. **$$**

Wedgewood Hotel & Spa 89.71
845 Homby St.;
800/663-0666;
wedgewoodhotel.com. **$$$**

VICTORIA
Ⓢ **Fairmont Empress** 88.05
866/540-4429;
fairmont.com. **$$**

WHISTLER
Fairmont Chateau Whistler 88.78
800/441-1414;
fairmont.com. **$$$**

Four Seasons Resort 92.74
800/332-3442;
fourseasons.com. **$$**

Ontario
OTTAWA
Fairmont Château Laurier 88.15
1 Rideau St.; 866/540-4410;
fairmont.com. **$$$**

TORONTO
Four Seasons Hotel 87.89
60 Yorkville Ave.;
800/332-3442; *fourseasons.com.* **$$$$**

Ritz-Carlton 92.00
181 Wellington St. W.;
800/241-3333;
ritzcarlton.com. **$$$$**

Quebec
MONTREAL
Ⓢ **Auberge du Vieux-Port** 89.20
97 Rue de la Commune E.;
888/660-7678;
aubergeduvieuxport.com. **$**

QUEBEC CITY
Auberge Saint-Antoine 90.71
8 Rue St.-Antoine; 888/692-2211; *saint-antoine.com.* **$$$**

Fairmont Le Château Frontenac 87.73
1 Rue des Carrières; 866/540-4460; *fairmont.com.* **$$**

The Caribbean, Bermuda + The Bahamas
Antigua
ST. JOHN'S
Curtain Bluff Resort 91.79
St. Ann; 888/726-3257;
888/289-9898;
curtainbluff.com. **$$$$$**

Galley Bay Resort & Spa 91.33
866/237-1644;
galleybayresort.com;
all-inclusive. **$$$$**

Rosewood Jumby Bay 89.83
888/767-3966;
rosewoodhotels.com;
all-inclusive. **$$$$$**

Bermuda
SOUTHAMPTON
Reefs Resort & Club 89.26
800/742-2008;
thereefs.com. **$$$$**

British Virgin Islands
VIRGIN GORDA
Rosewood Little Dix Bay 89.85
888/767-3966; *rosewood hotels.com.* **$$$$**

Cayman Islands
GRAND CAYMAN
Ritz-Carlton 89.20
800/241-3333;
ritzcarlton.com. **$$$$**

Jamaica
Couples Negril 90.17
Hanover; 800/268-7537;
couples.com; all-inclusive.
$$$$

Couples Sans Souci 88.32
St. Mary; 800/268-7537;
couples.com; all-inclusive.
$$$

Couples Swept Away 89.39
Westmoreland; 800/268-7537; *couples.com;*
all-inclusive. **$$$$**

Couples Tower Isle 89.91
St. Mary; 800/268-7537;
couples.com; all-inclusive.
$$$

Jamaica Inn 90.91
Ocho Rios; 800/837-4608;
jamaicainn.com. **$$$$**

Ⓢ **Rockhouse Hotel** 91.33
Negril; 876/957-4373;
rockhousehotel.com. **$**

Round Hill Hotel & Villas 88.40
Montego Bay; 800/972-2159; *roundhill.com.* **$$$$**

Sandals Royal Plantation 88.89
St. Ann; 888/726-3257;

Dining cliffside at Rockhouse Hotel, in Jamaica.

sandals.com; all-inclusive. **$$$$**

Nevis
Four Seasons Resort 90.48
Charlestown; 800/332-3442;
fourseasons.com. **$$$$**

Nisbet Plantation Beach Club 94.67
St. James Parish; 800/742-6008; nisbetplantation.com;
all-inclusive. **$$$$**

St. Bart's
Eden Rock 90.42
Baie de St.-Jean; 855/333-6762; edenrockhotel.com.
$$$$$

Hotel Saint-Barth Isle de France 90.89
Baie des Flamands; 800/810-4691; isle-de-france.com.
$$$$$

St. Lucia
Anse Chastanet 94.78
Soufrière; 800/223-1108;
ansechastanet.com. **$$$$**

Jade Mountain 95.33
Soufrière; 800/223-1108;
jademountain.com. **$$$$$**

Ladera Resort 90.35
Soufrière; 866/290-0978;
ladera.com. **$$$$**

Sandals Regency La Toc Golf Resort & Spa 87.80
Castries; 888/726-3257;
sandals.com. **$$$$**

Turks and Caicos
PROVIDENCIALES
Grace Bay Club 89.49
800/946-5757;
gracebayresorts.com. **$$$$$**

Key West Luxury Village at Beaches Turks & Caicos 89.65
888/232-2437;
beaches.com. **$$$$**

Seven Stars Resort 90.75
866/570-7777; sevenstars
gracebay.com. **$$$**

Somerset on Grace Bay 89.33
877/887-5722;
thesomerset.com. **$$$$**

U.S. Virgin Islands
ST. THOMAS
Ritz-Carlton 88.16
800/241-3333;
ritzcarlton.com. **$$$$**

Mexico

CANCÚN
Excellence Playa Mujeres 90.17
Quintana Roo; 866/540-2585; excellence-resorts.com;
all-inclusive. **$$$**

JW Marriott Cancún Resort & Spa 87.70
Km 14.5, Blvd. Kukulcan;
888/813-2776;
marriott.com. **$$**

Ritz-Carlton 90.68
36 Retorno del Rey; 800/241-3333; ritzcarlton.com. **$$$**

LOS CABOS
Capella Pedregal 93.81
Cabo San Lucas; 877/247-6688; capellahotels.com.
$$$$

Esperanza, an Auberge Resort 92.62
Cabo San Lucas; 866/311-2226; esperanzaresort.com.
$$$$

Las Ventanas al Paraíso, A Rosewood Resort 90.24
San José del Cabo;

888/767-3966;
rosewoodhotels.com. **$$$$**

One&Only Palmilla 92.26
San José del Cabo;
866/829-2977;
oneandonlyresorts.com. **$$$$**

Pueblo Bonito Los Cabos Resort 88.30
800/990-8250;
pueblobonito-loscabos.com;
all-inclusive. **$$$**

MAZATLÁN
Pueblo Bonito Emerald Bay Resort & Spa 91.83
800/990-8250; pueblobonito
emeraldbay.com; all-inclusive.
$$$

Pueblo Bonito Mazatlán Resort 92.94
800/990-8250;
pueblobonito-mazatlan.com;
all-inclusive. **$$$**

MEXICO CITY
Four Seasons Hotel México, D.F. 90.61
500 Paseo de la Reforma;
800/332-3442;
fourseasons.com. **$$$$**

PUERTO VALLARTA AREA
Grand Velas Riviera Nayarit 91.13
Nuevo Vallarta; 866/350-1487; grandvelas.com. **$$$$**

PUNTA MITA
Four Seasons Resort 88.91
800/332-3442;
fourseasons.com. **$$$$$**

St. Regis Punta Mita Resort 93.64
877/787-3447;
stregis.com. **$$$$**

RIVIERA MAYA
Banyan Tree Mayakoba 91.43
800/591-0439;
banyantree.com. **$$$$**

Grand Velas Riviera Maya 90.97
877/418-2963; rivieramaya.
grandvelas.com. **$$$$**

Maroma Resort & Spa by Orient-Express 89.57
866/454-9351;
maromahotel.com. **$$$$**

Rosewood Mayakoba 94.40
888/767-3966;
rosewoodhotels.com. **$$$$**

Secrets Maroma Beach Riviera Cancún 91.33
866/467-3273;
secretsresorts.com. **$$$$$**

ZIHUATANEJO
La Casa Que Canta 90.60
888/523-5050;
lacasaquecanta.com. **$$**

Central+ South America

Argentina
BARILOCHE
Llao Llao Hotel & Resort, Golf-Spa 89.88
800/223-6800;
llaollao.com.ar. **$$$**

BUENOS AIRES
Alvear Palace Hotel 93.77
1891 Avda. Alvear;
877/457-6315;
alvearpalace.com. **$$$$**

Four Seasons Hotel 91.23
1086/88 Calle Posadas;
800/332-3442;
fourseasons.com. **$$$$**

Palacio Duhau–Park Hyatt 90.18
1661 Avda. Alvear;
877/875-4658;
park.hyatt.com. **$$$$**

MENDOZA
Cavas Wine Lodge 94.80
54-261/410-6927;
cavaswinelodge.com. **$$$$**

Colombia
CARTAGENA
Sofitel Legend Santa Clara 90.53
800/763-4835;
sofitel.com. **$$$**

Costa Rica
ARENAL VOLCANO
NATIONAL PARK
Nayara Hotel, Spa & Gardens 96.14
La Fortuna; 866/311-1197;
arenalnayara.com. **$$$**

GUANACASTE
Four Seasons Resort Costa Rica at Peninsula Papagayo 92.13
800/332-3442;
fourseasons.com. **$$$$**

Ⓢ **Hotel Punta Islita** 92.00
866/446-4053;
hotelpuntaislita.com. **$$**

MANUEL ANTONIO
Arenas del Mar Beachfront & Rainforest Resort 90.67
888/240-0280;
arenasdelmar.com. **$$**

A guest suite at Hôtel Crillon le Brave, in Provence, France.

Ecuador

QUITO
Ⓢ **JW Marriott Hotel** 89.05
800/228-9290;
marriott.com. **$**

Peru

CUZCO
Hotel Monasterio by Orient-Express 91.14
136 Calle Palacio; 800/237-1236; *monasteriohotel.com.* **$$$$**

MACHU PICCHU PUEBLO
Inkaterra Machu Picchu Pueblo Hotel 89.60
800/442-5042;
inkaterra.com. **$$$$**

Europe

Austria

SALZBURG
Hotel Sacher 87.73
5-7 Schwarzstrasse; 43-662/889-770; *sacher.com.* **$$**

VIENNA
Hotel Imperial, a Luxury Collection Hotel 92.69
16 Kärntner Ring; 800/325-3589; *hotelimperialvienna.com.* **$$$$**

Hotel Sacher Wien 88.53
4 Philharmonikerstrasse;
43-1/514-560;
sacher.com. **$$$$**

Czech Republic

PRAGUE
The Augustine 93.33
Letenska; 800/745-8883;
theaugustine.com. **$$$$**

Four Seasons Hotel 90.18
2A/1098 Veleslavínova;
800/332-3442;
fourseasons.com. **$$$**

England

BATH
Royal Crescent Hotel & Spa 87.56
16 Royal Crescent;
800/735-2478;
royalcrescent.co.uk. **$$$**

BERKSHIRE
Cliveden House 89.33
Taplow; 44-1628/668-561;
clivedenhouse.co.uk. **$$$**

LONDON
The Athenaeum 89.41
116 Piccadilly; 800/335-3300;
athenaeumhotel.com. **$$**

The Berkeley 89.33
Wilton Place; 866/599-6991;
the-berkeley.co.uk. **$$$$**

Brown's Hotel 88.46
Albemarle St.; 888/667-9477; *roccofortehotels.com.*
$$$$

Chesterfield Mayfair 88.95
35 Charles St.; 877/955-1515; *chesterfieldmayfair.com.* **$$$**

Claridge's 90.69
Brook St.; 866/599-6991;
claridges.co.uk. **$$$$$**

The Connaught 92.36
Carlos Place; 866/599-6991;
the-connaught.co.uk. **$$$$**

Corinthia Hotel 92.24
Whitehall Place; 877/842-6269; *corinthia.com.* **$$$$**

Dukes St. James 87.56
35 St. James's Place;
800/381-4702;
dukeshotel.com. **$$**

41 90.67
41 Buckingham Palace Rd.;
877/955-1515;
41hotel.com. **$$$**

Four Seasons Hotel London at Park Lane 89.79
Hamilton Place, Park Lane,
800/332-3442;
fourseasons.com. **$$$$$**

The Goring 89.83
Beeston Place; 800/608-0273; *thegoring.com.* **$$$$**

The Lanesborough 89.44
Hyde Park Corner,
800/999-1828;
lanesborough.com. **$$$$**

The Langham 88.83
1C Portland Place,
Regent St.; 800/588-9141;
langhamhotels.com. **$$$$**

Mandarin Oriental Hyde Park 91.69
66 Knightsbridge;
800/526-6566;
mandarinoriental.com. **$$$$**

Milestone Hotel 91.82
1 Kensington Court;
800/223-6800;
milestonehotel.com. **$$$$**

The Ritz 91.09
150 Piccadilly;
877/748-9536;
theritzlondon.com. **$$$$**

Rubens at the Palace 90.10
39 Buckingham Palace Rd.;
877/955-1515;
rubenshotel.com. **$$**

The Savoy 90.67
Strand; 888/265-0533;
fairmont.com. **$$$$**

Stafford London by Kempinski 94.37
16-18 St. James's Place;
800/426-3135;
kempinski.com. **$$$$**

OXFORDSHIRE
Le Manoir aux Quat' Saisons 88.27
Great Milton; 800/237-1236; *manoir.com.* **$$$$$**

France

CÔTE D'AZUR
Château de la Chèvre d'Or 89.47
Èze Village; 33-4/92-10-66-66; *chevredor.com.* **$$$**

Hôtel Château Eza 89.88
Èze Village; 33-4/93-41-12-24; *chateaueza.com.* **$$$**

Hôtel du Cap-Eden-Roc 88.50
Antibes; 33-4/93-61-39-01;
hotel-du-cap-eden-roc.com.
$$$$$

CÔTE D'OR AREA
Hôtel Le Cep 88.42
27 Rue Maufoux, Beaune;
800/688-0414;
hotel-cep-beaune.com. **$$**

PARIS
Four Seasons Hotel George V 92.18
31 Ave. George V;
800/332-3442;
fourseasons.com. **$$$$$**

Hôtel de Crillon 88.62
10 Place de la Concorde;
800/888-4747;
crillon.com. **$$$$$**

Hôtel Lancaster 89.60
7 Rue de Berri;
800/223-6800;
hotel-lancaster.com. **$$$$**

Hôtel Le Meurice 90.11
228 Rue de Rivoli;
800/650-1842; *dorchester collection.com.* **$$$$**

Hôtel Plaza Athénée 90.71
25 Ave. Montaigne;
800/650-1842;
dorchestercollection.com.
$$$$$

Rubens at the Palace — *(see above)*

InterContinental Paris-Le Grand 87.67
2 Rue Scribe; 877/834-3613;
intercontinental.com. **$$$**

Le Bristol 91.84
112 Rue du Faubourg
St.-Honoré; 800/745-8883;
lebristolparis.com. **$$$$$**

Park Hyatt Paris-Vendôme 89.06
5 Rue de la Paix; 877/875-4658; *park.hyatt.com.*
$$$$$

Ritz Paris 89.73
15 Place Vendôme;
33-1/43-16-30-30;
ritzparis.com. **$$$$$**

PROVENCE
Hôtel Crillon le Brave 90.53
Crillon-le-Brave; 800/735-2478; *crillonlebrave.com.*
$$$$

Ⓢ **Hôtel D'Europe** 91.85
Avignon; 33-4/90-14-76-76;
heurope.com. **$$**

La Mirande 90.75
Avignon; 33-4/90-14-20-20;
la-mirande.fr. **$$$$**

Oustau de Baumanière & Spa 90.00
Les Baux-de-Provence;
33-4/90-54-33-07;
oustaudebaumaniere.com. **$$**

Villa Gallici 89.22
Aix-en-Provence;
800/735-2478;
villagallici.com. **$$$$**

REIMS
Château les Crayères 93.24
33-3/26-24-90-00;
lescrayeres.com. **$$$**

VERSAILLES
Trianon Palace, a Waldorf Astoria Hotel 88.44
33-1/30-84-50-00;
waldorfastoria.com. **$$$$**

Germany

BADEN-BADEN
Brenners Park-Hotel & Spa 92.67
49-7221/9000;
brenners.com. **$$$$**

BERLIN
Hotel Adlon Kempinski 90.09
77 Unter den Linden;
800/426-3135;
kempinski.com. **$$**

Ritz-Carlton 96.00
3 Potsdamer Platz; 800/241-3333; *ritzcarlton.com.* **$$**

HAMBURG
Park Hyatt 91.47
8 Bugenhagenstrasse;
877/875-4658;
park.hyatt.com. **$$**

MUNICH
Hotel Vier Jahreszeiten Kempinski 89.75
17 Maximilianstrasse;
800/426-3135;
kempinski.com. **$$$**

Mandarin Oriental 93.25
1 Neuturmstrasse;
800/526-6566;
mandarinoriental.com. **$$$$**

ROTHENBURG OB DER TAUBER
Ⓢ **Hotel Eisenhut** 89.88
49-9861/7050;
eisenhut.com. **$**

Greece

ATHENS
Hotel Grande Bretagne, a Luxury Collection Hotel 89.95
A1 Vas. Georgiou St.;
800/325-3589;
grandebretagne.gr. **$$**

Hungary

BUDAPEST
Ⓢ **Budapest Marriott Hotel** 88.75
4 Apáczai Csere János U.;
888/236-2427;
marriott.com. **$**

Four Seasons Hotel Gresham Palace 95.52
5-6 Széchenyi István Tér;
800/332-3442;
fourseasons.com. **$$**

Ⓢ **Kempinski Hotel Corvinus** 90.40
7-8 Erzsébet Tér; 800/426-3135; *kempinski.com.* **$**

Ireland

COUNTY CLARE
Dromoland Castle Hotel & Golf Country Club 89.50
Newmarket on Fergus;
800/346-7007;
dromoland.ie. **$$$$**

COUNTY LIMERICK
Adare Manor Hotel & Golf Resort 87.90
Adare; 800/462-3273;
adaremanor.com. **$$$$**

COUNTY MAYO
Ashford Castle 93.17
Cong; 800/346-7007;
ashford.ie. **$$$$**

COUNTY WATERFORD
Waterford Castle Hotel
88.94
Waterford; 353-51/878-203;
waterfordcastle.com. **$$**

COUNTY WICKLOW
**Powerscourt Hotel
(fomerly the Ritz-Carlton
Powerscourt)**
89.47
Enniskerry; 800/241-3333;
ritzcarlton.com. **$$$**

DUBLIN
Merrion Hotel 88.55
Upper Merrion St.;
800/223-6800;
merrionhotel.com. **$$**

**Shelbourne Dublin, a
Renaissance Hotel** 88.08
27 St. Stephen's Green;
800/228-9290;
marriott.com. **$$**

Westbury Hotel 91.24
Grafton St.; 800/223-6800;
lhw.com. **$$**

Italy
AMALFI COAST
Hotel Santa Caterina 92.74
Amalfi; 800/223-6800;
hotelsantacaterina.com.
$$$$

Il San Pietro di Positano
92.28
Positano; 800/735-2478;
ilsanpietro.it. **$$$$**

Le Sirenuse 92.31
Positano; 800/223-6800;
sirenuse.it. **$$$$**

**Palazzo Avino (formerly
Palazzo Sasso)** 93.60
Ravello; 39-089/818-181;
palazzoavino.com. **$$$**

ASOLO
Hotel Villa Cipriani 87.78
39-0423/523-411;
villaciprianiasolo.com. **$$**

CAPRI
Grand Hotel Quisisana
89.76
800/223-6800;
quisisana.com. **$$$**

CASOLE D'ELSA
**Castello di Casole-a
Timbers Resort** 96.18
888/548-9429;
castellodicasole.com. **$$$**

FLORENCE
**Four Seasons
Hotel Firenze** 91.73
99 Borgo Pinti;
800/332-3442;
fourseasons.com. **$$$$**

Hotel Brunelleschi 91.20
3 Piazza Santa Elisabetta;
39-055/27370;
hotelbrunelleschi.it. **$$**

Hotel Helvetia & Bristol
90.67
2 Via dei Pescioni;
800/223-6800;
*hotelhelvetiabristol
florence.com.* **$$**

Hotel Lungarno 90.31
14 Borgo San Jacopo;
39-055/2726-4000;
lungarnocollection.com.
$$$$

St. Regis 91.87
1 Piazza d'Ognissanti;
877/787-3447;
stregis.com. **$$$**

LAKE COMO
Villa d'Este 90.39
Cernobbio; 800/223-6800;
villadeste.com. **$$$$**

MILAN
Four Seasons Hotel Milano
90.14
6/8 Via Gesù; 800/332-
3442; *fourseasons.com.*
$$$$$

PORTOFINO
Hotel Spendido 88.91
800/237-1236;
hotelsplendido.com. **$$$$$**

ROME
Hotel de Russie 88.43
9 Via del Babuino;
888/667-9477;
roccofortehotels.com. **$$$$**

Hotel Hassler Roma 90.88
6 Piazza Trinità dei Monti;
800/223-6800;
hotelhasslerroma.com. **$$$$**

St. Regis 87.94
3 Via Vittorio Emanuele
Orlando; 877/787-3447;
stregis.com. **$$$**

SORRENTO
**Grand Hotel Excelsior
Vittoria** 91.45
34 Piazzo Tasso; 800/325-
8541; *exvitt.it.* **$$$**

VENICE
Bauers Il Palazzo 87.56
1459 San Marco; 800/223-
6800; *bauershotels.com.*
$$$$

**Gritti Palace, a Luxury
Collection Hotel** 88.41
2467 Campo Santa Maria del
Giglio; 800/325-3589;
starwoodhotels.com. **$$$$**

Hotel Cipriani 91.00
10 Giudecca; 800/237-1236;
hotelcipriani.com. **$$$$$**

Hotel Londra Palace 88.96
4171 Castello; 39-041/520-
0533; *londrapalace.com.* **$$**

**San Clemente Palace
Hotel & Resort (planned
reopening spring 2014)**
87.56
1 Isola di San Clemente.

Monaco
MONTE CARLO
Fairmont 89.78
12 Ave. des Spéluges;
800/441-1414;
fairmont.com. **$$$**

Hôtel de Paris 89.00
Place du Casino; 800/595-
0898; *hoteldeparismonte
carlo.com.* **$$$$**

Netherlands
AMSTERDAM
De l'Europe 88.84
2-14 Nieuwe Doelenstraat;
800/223-6800;
leurope.nl. **$$$**

Portugal
LISBON
Four Seasons Hotel Ritz
89.20
88 Rua Rodrigo da Fonseca;
800/332-3442;
fourseasons.com. **$$$**

Russia
ST. PETERSBURG
Grand Hotel Europe 89.18
1/7 Mikhailovskaya Ul.;
800/237-1236;
grandhoteleurope.com. **$$**

Scotland
EDINBURGH
The Balmoral 89.30
1 Princes St.; 888/667-9477;
roccofortehotels.com. **$$**

ST. ANDREWS
**Old Course Hotel, Golf
Resort & Spa** 87.60
800/223-6800;
oldcoursehotel.co.uk. **$$$**

Spain
BARCELONA
El Palace 90.35
668 Gran Via de les Corts
Catalanes; 800/223-6800;
hotelpalacebarcelona.com.
$$$$

Hotel Arts 89.68
19-21 Carrer de la Marina;
800/241-3333;
ritzcarlton.com. **$$$**

Mandarin Oriental 88.73
38 Passeig de Gràcia;
800/526-6567;
mandarinoriental.com. **$$$**

MADRID
Hotel Ritz 91.73
5 Plaza de la Lealtad;
800/237-1236;
ritzmadrid.com. **$$$**

Westin Palace 88.55
7 Plaza de las Cortes;
800/937-8461;
westin.com. **$$**

SEVILLE
**Hotel Alfonso XIII, a Luxury
Collection Hotel** 91.29
2 Calle San Fernando;
800/325-3589;
luxurycollection.com. **$$$**

Switzerland
ZURICH
Baur au Lac 89.88
1 Talstrasse; 800/223-6800;
bauraulac.ch. **$$$$**

Turkey
ISTANBUL
Çirağan Palace Kempinski
91.54
32 Çirağan Cad.; 800/426-
3135; *kempinski.com.* **$$$$**

**Four Seasons Hotel
Istanbul at Sultanahmet**
92.65
1 Tevkifhane Sk.; 800/332-
3442; *fourseasons.com.* **$$$**

**Four Seasons Hotel
Istanbul at the Bosphorus**
90.21
28 Çirağan Cad.; 800/332-
3442; *fourseasons.com.* **$$$**

ⓢ **Grand Hyatt** 93.60
1 Taskisla Cad.; 800/233-
1234; *grand.hyatt.com.* **$**

Ritz-Carlton 90.91
Suzer Plaza, 6 Askerocagi
Cad.; 800/241-3333;
ritzcarlton.com. **$$**

Africa + The Middle East

Botswana
MOREMI GAME RESERVE
**Mombo Camp and
Little Mombo Camp** 96.60
27-11/807-1800;
wilderness-safaris.com;
all-inclusive. **$$$$$**

Egypt
CAIRO
ⓢ **Four Seasons Hotel
Cairo at Nile Plaza** 94.00
1089 Corniche El Nil;
800/332-3442;
fourseasons.com. **$$**

ⓢ **Four Seasons Hotel
Cairo at the First
Residence** 92.53
35 Giza St.; 800/332-3442;
fourseasons.com. **$$**

ⓢ **Mena House
Oberoi** 90.24
Pyramids Rd.;
20-2/3377-3222;
menahousehotel.com. **$$$**

Israel
JERUSALEM
King David Hotel 87.93
23 King David St.; 800/223-
7773; *danhotels.com.* **$$$**

Jordan
AMMAN
ⓢ **Four Seasons Hotel**
93.60
5th Circle, Al-Kindi St.;
800/332-3442;
fourseasons.com. **$**

Kenya
AMBOSELI NATIONAL PARK
**Amboseli Serena Safari
Lodge** 88.96
254-20/284-2000;
serenahotels.com;
meals included. **$$$**

Tortilis Camp 91.00
254-20/600-3090; *tortilis.
com;* all-inclusive. **$$$$$**

**MASAI MARA NATIONAL
RESERVE**
**andBeyond Kichwa Tembo
Tented Camp** 94.53
877/421-2905; *andbeyond.
com;* all-inclusive. **$$$$$**

**Fairmont Mara
Safari Club** 91.20
800/441-1414;

KEY **$** *Less than $200*   **$$** *$200 to $350*   **$$$** *$350 to $500*   **$$$$** *$500 to $1,000*   **$$$$$** *More than $1,000*   ⓢ *Great Value ($250 or less)*

A regal living room at Adare Manor Hotel & Golf Resort, in Ireland.

fairmont.com; all-inclusive. **$$$$**

NAIROBI
Giraffe Manor 90.13
Koitobos Rd.; 254-725/675-830; *thesafaricollection.com*; meals included. **$$$$$**

NANYUKI
Fairmont Mount Kenya Safari Club 91.23
800/441-1414; *fairmont.com*; all-inclusive. **$$$$**

Morocco
MARRAKESH
La Mamounia 90.29
Ave. Bab Jdid; 800/223-6800; *mamounia.com*. **$$$$**

South Africa
CAPE TOWN
Cape Grace 94.55
W. Quay Rd.; 800/223-6800; *capegrace.com*. **$$$$**

Mount Nelson Hotel 91.50
76 Orange St.; 800/237-1236; *mountnelson.co.za*. **$$$**

One&Only 88.67
Dock Rd.; 888/877-7528; *oneandonlyresorts.com*. **$$$$**

Twelve Apostles Hotel & Spa 89.48
Victoria Rd.; 800/223-6800; *12apostleshotel.com*. **$$$$**

FRANSCHHOEK
Le Quartier Français 89.23
800/735-2478; *lqf.co.za*. **$$$**

JOHANNESBURG
Saxon Boutique Hotel, Villas & Spa 93.50
36 Saxon Rd.; 27-11/292-6000; *saxon.co.za*. **$$$$**

KRUGER NATIONAL PARK AREA
Londolozi Private Game Reserve 94.08
Sabi Sand Reserve; 27-11/280-6655; *londolozi.com*; all-inclusive. **$$$$$**

MalaMala Game Reserve 91.53
Sabi Sand Reserve; 27-11/442-2267; *malamala.com*; all-inclusive. **$$$$$**

Sabi Sabi Private Game Reserve 95.71
Sabi Sand Reserve; 27-11/447-7172; *sabisabi.com*; all-inclusive. **$$$$$**

Singita Kruger National Park 96.14
27-21/683-3424; *singita.com*; all-inclusive. **$$$$$**

Singita Sabi Sand 95.64
Sabi Sand Reserve; 27-21/683-3424; *singita.com*; all-inclusive. **$$$$$**

Tanzania
KARATU
Gibb's Farm 89.07
255-27/253-4397; *gibbsfarm.com*; meals included. **$$$$$**

NGORONGORO CRATER
andBeyond Ngorongoro Crater Lodge 91.11
877/421-2905; *andbeyond.com*; all-inclusive. **$$$$$**

Ngorongoro Sopa Lodge 89.09
255-27/250-0630; *sopalodges.com*; meals included. **$$$$**

SERENGETI NATIONAL PARK
Serengeti Serena Safari Lodge 88.71
255-28/262-1515; *serenahotels.com*; meals included. **$$$$**

United Arab Emirates
DUBAI
Burj Al Arab 90.51
Jumeirah Beach Rd.; 877/854-8051; *jumeirah.com*. **$$$$$**

Zambia
LIVINGSTONE
Royal Livingstone 90.80
260-21/332-1122; *suninternational.com*. **$$$$**

Asia
Burma
RANGOON
Governor's Residence 88.64
35 Taw Win Rd.; 800/237-1236; *governorsresidence.com*. **$$$$**

Cambodia
SIEM REAP
Amansara 94.18
Road to Angkor; 800/477-9180; *amanresorts.com*. **$$$$$**

La Résidence d'Angkor 91.17
River Rd.; 800/237-1236; *residencedangkor.com*. **$$$**

Raffles Grand Hotel d'Angkor 90.67
1 Vithei Charles de Gaulle; 800/768-9009; *raffles.com*. **$$**

Ⓢ **Sofitel Angkor Phokeethra Golf & Spa Resort** 92.57
Vithei Charles de Gaulle; 800/763-4835; *sofitel.com*. **$$**

Ⓢ **Victoria Angkor Resort & Spa** 88.25
855-63/760-428; *victoriahotels.asia*. **$$**

China
BEIJING
Park Hyatt 88.46
2 Jianguomenwai St.; 877/875-4658; *park.hyatt.com*. **$$$**

Peninsula Beijing 90.79
8 Goldfish Lane; 866/382-8388; *peninsula.com*. **$$$$**

Ⓢ **Regent** 90.25
99 Jinbao St.; 866/630-5890; *regenthotels.com*. **$**

Ritz-Carlton, Financial Street 93.00
1 Jin Cheng Fang St. E.,

Financial St.; 800/241-3333; *ritzcarlton.com*. **$$$**

Ⓢ **Shangri-La Hotel** 91.24
29 Zizhuyuan Rd.; 866/565-5050; *shangri-la.com*. **$**

St. Regis 90.67
21 Jianguomenwai Dajie; 877/787-3447; *stregis.com*. **$$$$**

Westin Beijing Financial Street 89.40
9B Financial St., Xicheng; 800/228-3000; *westin.com*. **$$**

GUILIN
Ⓢ **Shangri-La Hotel** 88.95
111 Huan Cheng Bei Er Rd.; 866/565-5050; *shangri-la.com*. **$$**

HONG KONG
Conrad 90.00
Pacific Place, 88 Queensway; 800/266-7237; *conradhotels.com*. **$$$$**

Four Seasons Hotel 90.13
International Finance Center, 8 Finance St.; 800/332-3442; *fourseasons.com*. **$$$$**

InterContinental 89.09
18 Salisbury Rd.; 800/327-0200; *intercontinental.com*. **$$$**

Island Shangri-La 91.47
Pacific Place, Supreme Court Rd.; 866/565-5050; *shangri-la.com*. **$$$**

Mandarin Oriental 94.18
5 Connaught Rd.; 800/526-6566; *mandarinoriental.com*. **$$$$**

The Langham 91.06
8 Peking Rd.; 800/588-9141; *langhamhotels.com*. **$$$**

Peninsula Hong Kong 94.88
Salisbury Rd.; 866/382-8388; *peninsula.com*. **$$$$**

LIJIANG
Banyan Tree 89.90
800/591-0439; *banyantree.com*. **$$$$**

SHANGHAI
Four Seasons Hotel 88.95
500 Weihai Rd.; 800/332-3442; *fourseasons.com*. **$$**

JW Marriott Hotel Shanghai at Tomorrow Square 90.29
399 Nanjing W. Rd.;

Impeccably
landscaped gardens
at Rambagh
Palace, in India.

800/228-9290;
marriott.com. **$$$**

Park Hyatt 90.53
100 Century Ave.;
877/875-4658;
park.hyatt.com. **$$$**

Peninsula Shanghai 94.18
32 Zhongshan Dong Yi Rd.;
866/382-8388;
peninsula.com. **$$$**

**Pudong Shangri-La East
Shanghai** 90.71
33 Fu Cheng Rd.; 866/565-
5050; *shangri-la.com.* **$$**

Westin Bund Center 90.20
88 Henan Central Rd.;
800/228-3000;
westin.com. **$$$$**

India
AGRA
Oberoi Amarvilas 93.44
Taj E. Gate Rd.; 800/562-
3764; *oberoihotels.com.*
$$$$

JAIPUR
Oberoi Rajvilas 94.84
Goner Rd.; 800/562-3764;
oberoihotels.com. **$$$$**

Rambagh Palace 91.76
Bhawani Singh Rd.;
866/969-1825;
tajhotels.com. **$$$$**

JODHPUR
Umaid Bhawan Palace
95.33
Circuit House Rd.;
866/969-1825;
tajhotels.com. **$$$$**

MUMBAI
Taj Mahal Palace 93.02
Apollo Bunder; 866/969-
1825; *tajhotels.com.* **$$**

Ⓢ **The Oberoi** 92.71
Sir Dorab Tata Rd., Nariman
Point; 800/562-3764;
oberoihotels.com. **$$**

NEW DELHI
The Imperial 88.10
1 Janpath; 800/323-7500;
theimperialindia.com. **$$**

The Oberoi 89.53
Dr. Zakir Hussain Marg;
800/562-3764;
oberoihotels.com. **$$$**

Oberoi, Gurgaon 93.33
443 Udyog Vihar;
800/562-3764;
oberoihotels.com. **$$**

Taj Mahal Hotel 89.78
1 Mansingh Rd.; 866/969-
1825; *tajhotels.com.* **$$**

UDAIPUR
Oberoi Udaivilas 95.73
Haridasji Ki Magri;
800/562-3764;
oberoihotels.com. **$$$$**

Taj Lake Palace 94.50
Lake Pichola; 866/969-1825;
tajhotels.com. **$$$$**

Japan
TOKYO
Peninsula Tokyo 93.11
1-8-1 Yuraku-cho;
866/382-8388;
peninsula.com. **$$$$**

Ritz-Carlton 90.40
9-7-1 Akasaka, Chiyoda-ku;
800/241-3333;
ritzcarlton.com. **$$$**

Laos
LUANG PRABANG
La Résidence Phou Vao
94.53
800/237-1236; *residence
phouvao.com.* **$$$$**

Malaysia
KUALA LUMPUR
Ⓢ **Shangri-La Hotel** 88.00
11 Jalan Sultan Ismail;
866/565-5050;
shangri-la.com. **$**

Philippines
BORACAY
Discovery Shores 95.57
63-2/720-8888; *discovery
hotels-resorts.com.* **$$**

**Shangri-La's Boracay
Resort & Spa** 89.92
866/565-5050;
shangri-la.com. **$$$$**

CEBU
**Shangri-La's Mactan
Resort & Spa** 89.63
866/565-5050;
shangri-la.com. **$$**

MANILA
Makati Shangri-La 89.41
Corner of Ayala Ave. and
Makati Ave., Makati City;
866/565-5050;
shangri-la.com. **$$**

Ⓢ **Peninsula Manila** 89.19
Corner of Ayala Ave. and
Makati Ave., Makati City;
866/382-8388;
peninsula.com. **$**

Singapore
Fullerton Bay Hotel 92.44
80 Collyer Quay;
65/6333-8388;
fullertonbayhotel.com. **$$$**

Fullerton Hotel 88.71
1 Fullerton Square;
65/6733-8388;
fullertonhotel.com. **$$**

Grand Hyatt 89.80
10 Scotts Rd.; 800/233-
1234; *grand.hyatt.com.* **$$$**

Mandarin Oriental 89.42
5 Raffles Ave.;
800/526-6566;
mandarinoriental.com. **$$$**

Raffles 88.62
1 Beach Rd.; 800/768-9009;
raffles.com. **$$$$$**

Ritz-Carlton, Millenia
89.60
7 Raffles Ave.; 800/241-
3333; *ritzcarlton.com.* **$$$$**

St. Regis 91.11
29 Tanglin Rd.; 877/787-
3447; *stregis.com.* **$$$**

South Korea
SEOUL
Grand Hyatt 87.78
322 Sowol-ro; 800/233-
1234; *grand.hyatt.com.* **$$**

Thailand
BANGKOK
Ⓢ **Four Seasons Hotel**
90.36
155 Rajadamri Rd.;
800/332-3442;
fourseasons.com. **$$**

Ⓢ **Grand Hyatt Erawan**
89.11
494 Rajdamri Rd.;
800/233-1234;
grand.hyatt.com. **$**

Ⓢ **JW Marriott Hotel**
91.29
4 Sukhumvit Rd.; 800/228-
9290; *jwmarriott.com.* **$$**

Mandarin Oriental 94.47
48 Oriental Ave.;
800/526-6566;
mandarinoriental.com. **$$$**

Peninsula Bangkok 92.87
333 Charoennakorn Rd.;
866/382-8388;
peninsula.com. **$$$$**

Ⓢ **Royal Orchid Sheraton
Hotel & Towers** 90.11
2 Charoen Krung Rd.;

800/325-3535;
sheraton.com. **$**

Ⓢ **Shangri-La Hotel** 91.12
89 Soi Wat Suan Plu,
New Rd.; 866/565-5050;
shangri-la.com. **$**

**Sheraton Grande
Sukhumvit, a Luxury
Collection Hotel** 90.00
250 Sukhumvit Rd.;
800/325-3589;
sheraton.com. **$$**

CHIANG MAI
Four Seasons Resort 91.59
800/332-3442;
fourseasons.com. **$$$$**

Dhara Dhevi 93.76
66-53/88-8888;
dharadhevi.com. **$$$$**

PHUKET
**JW Marriott Phuket
Resort & Spa** 88.89
800/228-9290;
marriott.com. **$$**

Vietnam
HANOI
Sofitel Legend Metropole
93.33
15 Ngo Quyen St.; 800/
763-4835; *sofitel.com.* **$$**

HO CHI MINH CITY
Park Hyatt Saigon 91.13
2 Lam Son Square;
877/875-4658;
park.hyatt.com. **$$**

HOI AN
Nam Hai 91.71
84-51/394-0000;
thenamhaihaihoian.com.
$$$$

HUE
Ⓢ **La Résidence Hue Hôtel
& Spa** 88.46
5 Lê Loi St., Vĩnh Ninh;
84-54/383-7475;
la-residence-hue.com. **$**

Australia,
New
Zealand,+
The South
Pacific

Australia
GREAT BARRIER REEF
**One&Only Hayman Island
(formerly Hayman)** 91.11
Hayman Island;

800/745-8883;
oneandonlyresorts.com.
$$$$

MELBOURNE
The Langham
89.60
1 Southgate Ave.;
800/588-9141;
langhamhotels.com. **$$$**

SYDNEY
InterContinental
88.22
117 Macquarie St.;
800/327-0200;
intercontinental.com. **$$**

Park Hyatt 88.15
7 Hickson Rd.; 877/875-
4658; *park.hyatt.com.* **$$$$**

Shangri-La Hotel 88.36
176 Cumberland St.;
866/565-5050;
shangri-la.com. **$$**

French Polynesia
BORA-BORA
Four Seasons Resort
96.00
Motu Tehotu; 800/332-3442;
fourseasons.com. **$$$$**

St. Regis 91.61
Motu Ome'e; 877/787-3447;
stregis.com. **$$$$$**

New Zealand
MATAURI BAY
Lodge at Kauri Cliffs 96.00
64-9/407-0010;
kauricliffs.com;
all-inclusive. **$$$$$**

TAUPO
Huka Lodge 93.07
64-7/378-5791;
hukalodge.com;
all-inclusive. **$$$$$**

A citrus drink at
the Cocktail
Terrace at 21c
Museum Hotel,
in Cincinnati.

Trips Directory

The cozy lounge
area at Casa Chic,
in Uruguay.

Index

Assorted knickknacks at Basecamp Hotel, in Colorado.

284

Contributors

Kate Appleton

Aimee Lee Ball

Luke Barr

Colin Barraclough

Andrea Bennett

Vinita Bharadwaj

Laura Begley Bloom

Jacki Caradonio

Aric Chen

Jennifer Chen

Fiona Donnelly

Robyn Eckhardt

Nikki Ekstein

Amy Farley

Rachel Felder

Andrew Ferren

Jennifer Flowers

Peter J. Frank

Jaime Gillin

Adam Graham

Darrell Hartman

Frances Hibbard

Katie James

Brooke Porter Katz

David A. Keeps

Stirling Kelso

Brian Kevin

Sarah Khan

Matt Lee

Ted Lee

Melanie Lieberman

Peter Jon Lindberg

Alexandra Marshall

J.J. Martin

Heidi Mitchell

Shane Mitchell

Bob Morris

Mark Morrison

Sheila Ortona-Pierce

Kathryn O'Shea-Evans

Sophy Roberts

Bruce Schoenfeld

Clara O. Sedlak

Kate Sekules

Andrew Sessa

Patrick Sheehan

Maria Shollenbarger

Gail Simmons

Paola Singer

Samai Singh

Sarah Spagnolo

Laura Teusink

Matt Villano

Hannah Wallace

Valerie Waterhouse

Ingrid Williams

Alexandra Wolfe

Peering over
the pool at
Taj Mahal Palace,
in Mumbai.

Photographers